UNDER THE SOUTHERN CROSS

UNDER THE SOUTHERN CROSS

© 2000, Jeffrey Picknicki Morski

All rights reserved. No part of this book may be reproduced, stored in a retrieval system or transmitted in any form or by any means without written permission from Watson & Dwyer Publishing, an imprint of J. Gordon Shillingford Publishing Inc., except for brief excerpts used in critical reviews, for any reason, by any means, without the permission of the publisher.

Cover and interior design by Doowah Design Inc.
Printed and bound in Canada

We acknowledge the financial support of the Manitoba Arts Council
and The Canada Council for the Arts for our publishing program.

UNDER THE SOUTHERN CROSS
A Collection of Accounts and Reminiscences about the Ukrainian Immigration in Brazil, 1891-1914
Jeffrey Picknicki Morski

Photograph of Dr. Yosyf Oleskiv (National Archives of Canada, C-009366)

Photographs of São Paulo Railway's Paranapiacaba Station
    and the port of Santos (Museu da Imigração, São Paulo)

Photographs on pages 13, 25, 32, 34, 35, 41, 43, 50, 54, 55
    (Petro Karmansky, *Mizh ridnymy v Pivdennii Amerytsi*)

Map of Ilha das Flores, Rio de Janeiro, Brazil
    (Arquivo Nacional, Coordenação de Acesso à Informação, Rio de Janeiro)

The maps on pages iii, vi and vii were produced by Welden Heibert,
    Cartography Office, University of Winnipeg

Footer: "Do Brazylii" ("To Brazil") and "Lyst iz Brazylii" ("Letter from Brazil"), poetry by Ivan
    Franko (in Ukrainian), published in Lviv, 1898.

Canadian Cataloguing in Publication Data

Morski, Jeffrey Picknicki

    Under the Southern Cross: a collection of accounts and
reminiscences about the Ukrainian immigration in Brazil, 1891-1914

Includes bibliographical references.
ISBN 1-896239-62-5

    1. Ukrainians—Brazil—History. 2. Brazil—Emigration
and immigration—History. 3. Ukraine—Emigration and
immigration—History. I. Title.

F2659.U4M67 2000   981'.600491791   C00-900173-5

TABLE OF CONTENTS

PREFACE i

INTRODUCTION iii

CHAPTER 1
About Free Lands by Dr. Yosyf Oleskiv 1

CHAPTER 2
About Emigration by Dr. Yosyf Oleskiv 7

CHAPTER 3
The First to Arrive by João Pacevicz 11

CHAPTER 4
Our Beginnings in Rio Claro by Teodoro Potoskei 15

CHAPTER 5
Memories from the First Waves of Emigration by André Hotzailuk 23

CHAPTER 6
In Search of a Better Life by Felipe Kobrên 29

CHAPTER 7
In the Paths of Many by Miguel Cheuczuk 39

CHAPTER 8
And for the meal pyrohy and piranhas by Luca Morski 47

CHAPTER 9
Among Our People in South America by Petro Karmansky 53

CHAPTER 10
We Cooked the Chicken Seven Times by Luca Morski 59

CHAPTER 11
Letters Home by Pedro Veltchevski, Fedorko Mechalovsky, João Petrovitch 61

CHAPTER 12
To Find My Father by Paulo Muzêka 65

ENDNOTES 75

SELECTED BIBLIOGRAPHY 82

PREFACE

Over 100 years have passed since the arrival of the first Ukrainians in Brazil. Their emigration brought some 45,000 pioneers to settle in the Brazilian South between the years 1891 and 1914, a small number of the more than 500,000 who would come to make their home in the Americas during this period. As with the movement to Canada, it was the search for a better life for themselves and a more prosperous legacy for those who would come after them—not the blinding poverty and rigid oppression as is still perpetuated by mythology—which led to this mass migration of individuals, families and sometimes even whole villages to the New World. What was their journey like? What were their first thoughts and impressions as they arrived in Brazil? Would they find what they were looking for? How did they adjust to an environment and social structure which were so different from their own? Would they regret their decisions?

The following collection of accounts and reminiscences about the first wave of Ukrainian emigration to Brazil provides answers to some of these questions. Forgotten and long buried in archives, libraries, family scrapbooks and the pages of the Ukrainian-Brazilian press, the writings have preserved a valuable link to the past. They are the immigrants' stories in their own words, told as only they could tell them and with all the colour, flavour and emotion that first-hand accounts provide. Presented here for the first time in English translation, they offer the reader the ability to further understand and appreciate the collective courage, sacrifice and determination that was the pioneer experience.

The selection of stories to include within this volume was not a difficult one to make. The descriptive accounts by André Hotzailuk and Felipe Kobrên provide little-known details about the trans-Atlantic crossing, the much anticipated Brazilian arrival and the time spent in the immigration barracks. The memoirs of Luca Morski tell of the difficulties of settling in and adapting to the new Brazilian environment. Teodoro Potoskei, João Pacevicz and Miguel Cheuczuk offer details of pride, progress and accomplishment. Paulo Muzêka's story is representative of those of a number of young men who were detained or prevented from emigrating because of unfulfilled military obligations. Those by Oleskiv and Karmansky, written not as immigrants but from the perspective of the Ukrainian intelligentsia, offer further insight and information about the immigrant experience in Brazil.

As important as the information they impart are the myths and misconceptions which the writings of the settlers serve to dispel. As their stories suggest, the Ukrainian immigrants did not fit the model of the backward country bumpkins of popular belief. They were peasants of some means—typically with an elementary school education, skilled in various trades and crafts and possessing a depth of character and personality—who almost at once undertook to build churches, schools and found cultural organizations in Brazil. Furthermore, their emigration was not a desperate escape from the misery of the homeland but an attempt at securing for themselves a more prosperous future as they recognized the ever-growing limitations of life in Galicia. Throughout, it is the search for something better, the hard work and determination of the settlers and the *saudades*, a Portuguese word meaning unbearable sadness and longing for all that was left behind, which emerge as pervasive themes.

The stories presented certain challenges, if not difficulties, in their translation from Ukrainian. The high incidence of Galician dialectisms, Polish-language borrowings and linguistic innovations from Portuguese in the language of the pioneers needed special attention in order to insure an accurate translation. It required a certain *jeito*, as the Brazilians call their knack or aptitude for working through problems, to make the necessary adaptations to English so that the spirit of the thought would not be lost. There were some references in the text which needed further identification or explanation for the modern reader, especially from the realms of Brazilian-Portuguese regional and technical vocabulary and the Ukrainian folk calendar of celebrations, rites and rituals. This was solved by the preparation, as required, of explanatory endnotes.

In all cases, while the stories have been adapted for style, clarity and readability, they remain true to their original in essence if not exactly in form. Liberties were taken with the translations only when necessary. Potoskei's repeated references to what he saw as the shortcomings of his fellow Polish immigrants, for example, detracted from the text and were abbreviated. Kobrên's social commentaries were extraneous to the descriptions of the immigrant experience and have been omitted. The authors' individual writing styles, which varied greatly from the simple sentences of some to the highly eloquent prose of others, have nonetheless been left unaltered. In rendering Ukrainian words into English I have used the Modified Library of Congress System of Cyrillic Transliteration with the following variants: я-ya, ю-yu, є-ye, ї-yi and й-y when occurring initially.

This book would not have been possible without the help and contributions of numerous people. My family, friends and colleagues in Rio de Janeiro, Curitiba and Prudentópolis, Brazil, with whom I have lived and worked on numerous occasions, have continued to offer their assistance, support and encouragement throughout the over 15 years I have spent researching and writing about the history of the Ukrainian immigration in Brazil.

Among those in Prudentópolis, I owe a lifetime of gratitude to Father Pedro Baltzar, OSBM, and Sister Eumélia Tarnovskei, of the Comitê Social de Ajudas do Fundo Agrário de UUARC, for their help and contributions dating to 1981.

I am grateful to Maria Lurdes Kassiano for her assistance in photocopying archival materials and to Father Tarcísio Zaluski, OSBM, editor of *Prácia*, and dona Nadir Julek, at the press, for providing unrestricted access to the newspaper's archives.

I offer my most sincere thanks and appreciation to Father Atanásio Kupinski, OSBM, for permitting me to use some photographs from his personal collection herein.

I remain eternally grateful to my cousin and *grande amiga* Nádia Morskei Stasiu, Prudentópolis's past Secretary of Tourism, for the help, support, friendship, loyalty and hospitality which she unfailingly provides me. Serei eternamente grato à minha prima e grande amiga, Nádia Morskei Stasiu, ex-Secretária de Turismo de Prudentópolis, pela sua inesgotável ajuda, apoio, amizade, lealdade e hospitalidade. Muitíssimo obrigado! Eu adoro você!

Antônio Carlos G. Valerio, of the Arquivo Nacional in Rio de Janeiro, provided valuable assistance in obtaining information from the registry books of immigrants at Ilha das Flores. Mauro Guimarães, of Rio de Janeiro, and the late Nestor Kutenskei, of the Sociedade dos Amigos da Cultura Ucraniana in Curitiba, provided me the opportunity of tracing the steps of the immigrants at Rio's Ilha das Flores, the port of Paranaguá, Paraná, and then continuing the pilgrimage inland along the Caminho do Itupava to Curitiba and Prudentópolis.

I also wish to thank Myroslava Diadiuk of Lviv's Tsentralnyi Derzhavnyi Istorychnyi Arkhiv (Central State Historical Archive) for her assistance during my research work in Ukraine, especially in preparing materials and helping to locate elusive files.

Closer to home, I am grateful to Prof. John C. Lehr and Orysia Tracz of Winnipeg for reading the manuscript and offering their critiques. Prof. Lehr, it must also be said, provided the initial idea and the title for this book. His help, support and encouragement have made the transition from manuscript to monograph a considerably easier process. My deepest *muito obrigado* is extended to Prof. Serhii Cipko of the Department of History and Classics, University of Alberta, for first introducing me to the Ukrainians in Brazil those many years ago, assisting me immeasurably in the search for my extended family in Paraná and, most recently, for reading the manuscript and providing valuable suggestions, changes and improvements.

The publication of this book would not have been possible without the assistance of the Petro Jacyk Educational Foundation in Mississauga, Ontario. I am grateful to Mr. Jacyk and Dr. Marko Stech, the Foundation's Managing Director, for their very generous financial support.

Finalmente, agradeço a todos que participaram e contribuiram na preparação deste livro, pela ajuda inestimável, especialmente durante a minha pesquisa e estadia no Brasil, pelo apoio e encorajamento generoso com o qual eu sempre pude contar, aos meus familiares e amigos no Rio de Janeiro, em Curitiba e Prudentópolis, cuja ajuda e hospitalidade estimo tanto e nunca poderei retribuir, eu fico sinceramente agradecido.

JPM

INTRODUCTION

In the late 1800s Ukrainians began looking towards the Americas in their search for a better life for themselves and their families. It was the New World which offered them hope for the future when their Galician homeland could no longer support and sustain its people. Overcrowding in the countryside, a shortage of cropland, limited employment opportunities and a society which was unable to encourage and promote their potential had forced them to look elsewhere. For many Ukrainians, Brazil was the promised land. As they left in what would be the paths of many—through different European countries, Italian or German ports of departure and across the Atlantic Ocean to South America—it was a journey which would take them some 6,000 miles from their native villages to a new life a whole world away.

TO BRAZIL

The year 1891 is traditionally regarded as the beginning of the Ukrainian emigration to Brazil. The actual mass emigration, however, began four years later in 1895 and continued until the outbreak of World War I in 1914. This first wave, with numbers between 40,000 and 45,000, was comprised almost exclusively of Ukrainians of East Galician origin, specifically from the counties of Berezhany, Bibrka, Brody, Buchach, Chesaniv, Chortkiv, Drohobych, Kamianka Strumylova, Lviv, Peremyshliany, Pidhaitsi, Rava Ruska, Rohatyn, Skalat, Sniatyn, Sokal, Terebovlia, Ternopil, Tovmach, Zalishchyky, Zbarazh, Zhovkva and Zolochiv. The second and third waves of emigration were considerably smaller than the influx of new arrivals to 1914 and brought no more than 9,000 Ukrainians in the interwar years and approximately 7,000 from Displaced Persons camps in Western Europe following the end of World War II.

It was on the initiative of the Brazilian government that the immigration movement began. Faced with the impending abolition of Afro-Brazilian slavery, the authorities looked towards the recruitment and settlement in Brazil of Europeans as a potential new source of labour, especially for the coffee and rubber plantations. Furthermore, inspired by programs of immigration and colonization which were being undertaken by the governments in North America at the time, Brazil saw immigration as a means of opening and settling the country's sparsely populated southern frontier regions.

Beginning in the late 1880s, Brazilian government and also privately sponsored immigration and steamship agents, the latter predominantly from Italy, were dispatched across Central and Eastern Europe in order to bring the immigrants to Brazil. Telling of free land, high wages and even of "streets paved with emeralds," they encouraged and enticed the people into leaving for the New World. In fact the incentives of paid passage and land concessions, which were initially offered to prospective immigrants by the Brazilian government, were suspended in late 1895, although many Europeans were led to Brazil by the actions of duplicitous agents who continued to make these and other false promises. The campaigns, while initially aimed towards the Poles, gradually reached the Ukrainian peasantry of East Galicia where the emigration movement to Brazil was particularly strong.

The Counties of East Galicia, 1891

THE FIRST IMMIGRANTS, 1891-1914

It was not long after the recruitment began that the "Brazilian Fever," as it came to be called, seized much of the Ukrainian rural population. From Sokal to Sniatyn immigration agents and those representing European steamship companies spoke at meetings and other public gatherings about the opportunities of a new life in Brazil. Their enthusiastic and often impassioned speeches, many of which misrepresented the realities of settlement in Brazil, quickly captivated the villagers and turned their initial interest in the prospect of relocating to South America into a frenzy of misinformed decisions and hasty departures. In the spring of 1894 it was reported in the Ukrainian newspaper *Batkivshchyna* that:

> The emigration fever has taken on such proportions that it is hardly possible to deal with the people in the countryside. Everyday they come for advice, asking, "What is the best way for us to get to Brynzolia?" Naturally, the reply from any intelligent person is always the same—do not leave your native land—but it is of no help because they are being encouraged to emigrate by the greedy profiteers, especially the Jews. The reason for the fury of emigration fever has been identified many times before but I will say it here again—the poverty, the utter poverty!

When the authorities saw that the people were leaving their homes, not knowing what would be waiting for them in Brazil, they started thinking about what could be done. Some of the men said that the people should be detained forcibly, refused passports and those attempting to leave turned back at the border. Others said that this would only worsen the situation. The people will continue to leave, they explained, and be faced with even more difficulties in the New World without any money at all. A better idea would be to find out more about Brazil and the conditions in which our people are living...

Several of our officials travelled to Brazil and described what they saw. They tell that the country is comprised of 20 states, 16 of which are so terribly hot that the immigrants are dying from the high temperatures and yellow fever. The forests, in which even ferns grow to be as tall as trees, are full of monstrous snakes and wild animals. Only the three states in the very south of Brazil, where it is possible to cultivate our European crops, are spared the eternal heat and disease. The Brazilian government no longer gives out free land to the people settling in the colonies of Paraná. Land is now purchased on payments with prices of several *zoloti rynski* for a *morg* of unbroken forest. The initial work on the land is very difficult because you first have to clear this endless forest, the likes of which you have never seen, my good man, and which you will never see back home! Many did

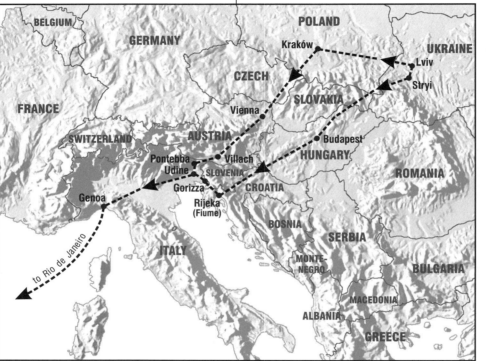

Departure Routes for Ukrainians Emigrating to Brazil through the port of Genoa, 1891-1914

not survive the work in clearing the land and have perished (en route and already in Brazil) with almost one-quarter of the settlers dead or dying, especially young children and older men and women... (*Batkivshchyna*, April 1 (13), 1894)

Alarmed by such reports, the local government and members of the Ukrainian intelligentsia undertook a number of different measures to stop or divert the emigration movement. In 1895 the *starostvo*, or captaincy, in each of the counties in East Galicia began sending out announcements to all members of the Ukrainian Catholic clergy in which they described in detail the dangers of settling in Brazil. These were to be read aloud in church in an effort to alert and inform prospective emigrants. The gendarmerie was instructed to prevent anyone suspected of leaving for Brazil from buying train tickets to any destination. Warnings also appeared in the newspapers, as in this open letter to the people from Dr. Yosyf Oleskiv of Lviv who was particularly concerned with the problems facing the Ukrainian peasantry and their plans to emigrate to Brazil. It reads, in part:

> Of all the countries in the world where our people can settle, Brazil is the least desirable and emigration there will mean complete and certain doom. It is the offer of free land and paid passage which is drawing our people to Brazil but, in truth, the land is not given out for free...
>
> The Brazilian government has recently ended its program of colonization in the province [sic] of Paraná where our people have been settling up until now. Those who go to Brazil will no longer find themselves on farms but will be contracted out to work as slaves on the coffee and cotton plantations. The wages are terrible, the work is extremely hard and our people cannot cope in such a hot and steamy climate. Yellow fever, a disease which is no less horrible than typhus or cholera, is raging rampantly through the country...
>
> The colonies in Paraná have no future. In order to sell their grain, our colonists would have to secure a market in Europe which is a month away by ship. And how would their product compare with that of the United States, Canada, Russia, India or southern Siberia? Paraná is connected to the coast by a single rail line whose tariffs are so terribly high that it is not profitable to transport grain but only a more valuable commodity like mate tea. The Brazilian and Argentine currency has been terribly devalued, the country's administration is lawless, it practises slavery and it simply does what it wants. The country has no trade of its own, duties on imported goods are high and the farmland is of the poorest quality... Add to this the raids by the savage Botocudo Indians, the large and poisonous snakes, yellow fever, jaguars and other wild jungle animals and there you have the concept of the famous Brazilian paradise. (*Batkivshchyna*, May 1 (13), 1894)

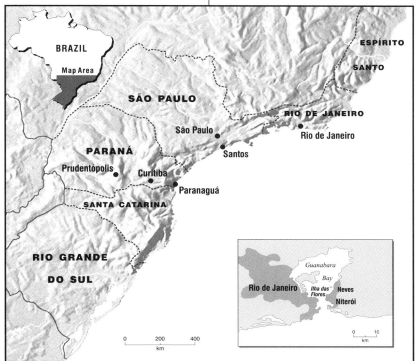

Brazil: The City of Rio de Janeiro, Guanabara Bay and the Southern Coastal States

Despite the warnings the Ukrainians continued to leave for Brazil and, for some, the consequences of their decisions appeared even before departing Europe. Many were cheated of their money by dishonest steamship agents and sub-agents who sold them counterfeit tickets or charged them for non-existent port and emigration taxes. Others were turned back at the Galician border because they failed to possess valid passports. Still others, having been equally misinformed about the emigration process, were left stranded at the Italian or German ports of departure for not having met all of the conditions necessary for emigration. Men, for example, were asked to show proof of having completed their military service (unless they were exempt) and passengers were required to have with them money for the trip, usually 50 *zoloti rynski* (about 25 Canadian dollars) per person, which they would be asked to produce for the officials prior to embarkation.

Upon arrival in Brazil the immigrants were first accommodated in barracks on the island of Ilha das Flores in Guanabara Bay near the city of Rio de Janeiro where they received food and shelter until the formalities of the arrival were completed. Transport to the settlement zones, usually by ship along the coast to the port of Paranaguá and then inland by train, was provided by the government. Alternatively, the immigrants travelled to barracks in Pinheiro, São Paulo, Curitiba or

One of the form letters (in Polish) sent by Silvio Nodari informing prospective emigrants of the suspension of free steamship passage to Brazil but continuing to offer emigration services for paying customers.

Prudentópolis, the centre of the colonization, to await the surveying and registering of the individual land parcels, called chácaras, in the Paraná interior. Some even trekked inland on foot from Paranaguá, some 60 kilometres following the Caminho do Itupava, an ancient trail across the Serra do Mar, to Curitiba. Life in the barracks, as long as a year for some, was harsh and many did not survive. The situation in Curitiba was among the worst.

> The conditions here are terrible. There is no law and order and no one dares to go outside to his neighbour at night without carrying a gun or a knife. Murder is commonplace and the police themselves are thieves. Everyone makes his own justice. (*Batkivshchyna*, July 1 (13), 1896)

Having claimed their land, the immigrants were directed to their places of settlement, travelling by mule or horse-drawn cart and typically at their own expense. It was a slow and arduous journey made even more difficult by the heat, insects, distance and fatigue. Paths would often have to be cut through the forest where none previously existed. Others needed to be widened so that the animals or carts could pass through. Colonization laws had provided for some initial support in the form of food, basic tools and temporary shelter in order to help the immigrants settle into their new surroundings. In many cases, however, the Ukrainians were abandoned and left to fend for themselves. They were extremely susceptible and succumbed to disease, especially yellow fever, while others died from starvation or exposure to the elements. Some perished in violent confrontations with the Brazilian Indians, as in the massacre of seven Ukrainian families at Costa Carvalho, Santa Catarina, in 1900. Many did not survive the first year. The death rate was extremely high and by 1897, barely two years after the beginning of the mass emigration, the cemetery in Prudentópolis had as many as 3,000 graves.

The pattern of settlement in Brazil was similar to that of the new arrivals in Canada; that is, the people settled in homogeneous groups or clusters which were often based on kinship or old-country village ties and almost exclusively in the rural frontier areas, especially among the first wave. These clusters, called *colônias* (colonies) or *linhas* (line villages), came to be a characteristic feature of Ukrainian settlement—and indeed of other European immigrant groups—in Brazil. They established new colonies and reinforced old ones with each arrival of new immigrants. For the overwhelming majority the settlement was confined to the states of Paraná, Santa Catarina and Rio Grande do Sul where even today, especially in the southeastern part of Paraná, there remains a strong Ukrainian presence.

UKRAINIAN LIFE IN BRAZIL

Kukurudza yak smereka, v liti zymno, v zymi speka. (The corn grows as tall as fir trees. The weather is cold in summer and hot in winter.) Clearly, as illustrated in this rhyming proverb from the early years of settlement, life in Brazil was not what many immigrants expected. Different in virtually every aspect from the land they left behind, there were numerous hardships and difficulties in making the transition to life in the New World. Coming from densely populated Eastern Europe, the Ukrainians found themselves in sparsely inhabited territory and extreme isolation in Brazil. The colonies were located mainly in heavily forested or jungle areas with neighbouring settlements typically situated a great distance apart. A subtropical climate, with its extreme summer heat, the absence of snow in winter and the antipodean seasons, required further adjustment. Everything was a new experience.

> I was 13 years old when we arrived in Brazil in 1897. In my wildest dreams I never expected it to be like this. When we came to Prudentópolis, my father was given a bag of black beans and we were placed in a cart and driven to our land. We stared at everything in amazement. The red soil, the pinheiros with their tufted branches and trunks as big as any one of our Galician houses, the brightly coloured parrots which the locals called *papagaio*. It was all so different.
>
> Before we could even unload the bags from the cart, a snake had made its way into our tent and scared my mother half to death. Father gathered branches and made a fire for us to cook some food. We were all alone. As we spent the first night in our new home, there was only the forest to hear our cries. In the sky above, the Southern Cross reminded us that God was watching over. (Paulo Krauczuk, 1932)

Predominantly agriculturalists, the Ukrainians in Brazil continued to make their livelihood from working the land. Certain changes and adaptations in the cultivation of traditional garden and field crops, however, would have to be made as a result of the new environment. Poppy and caraway, which grew well in Europe, initially did poorly in Brazil. Cucumbers and melons were susceptible to winter wind and frost and would not be planted between the months of April and August. Wheat was extremely vulnerable to birds and other predators and was seldom cultivated by the early settlers. Hemp would not grow in the iron-rich red soils. Black beans, *mandioca* (cassava), *batatas* (sweet potatoes), field rice, coffee, bananas and oranges were some of the new crops introduced by the Brazilians.

Further changes were made in traditional farming methods and practices. The old-world agricultural cycle, its rhythm and performance regulated by the seasons and replete with rites and rituals believed to insure a good harvest, was not suited to Brazil where there was no significant delineation between winter, spring, summer and fall. Planting could take place at any time during the year. Potatoes could be grown twice. Grains such as buckwheat could be sown and harvested three times. Hay was cut and dried as required. Most vegetables, legumes and cereals were cultivated year-round with new crops sown immediately following their harvest. Crop damage took on new proportions in the subtropics as ants, locusts and worms, the size and number of which did not exist in Europe, destroyed entire fields and gardens. Parrots, which were known to be especially destructive, were capable of ruining the yield of an entire orchard. Poisonous snakes, tarantulas and wild animals posed additional serious threats.

One of the greatest problems facing the people during the early years of settlement was the lack of their own priests and churches. Although the first Ukrainian priest arrived in Brazil in 1896, it was not until several years later that the number of clergy members grew and could begin to properly serve the religious and spiritual needs of the people. The Ukrainian Catholic Church and the Basilian missionaries have long played an important role in Ukrainian life in Brazil, not only in terms of fulfilling their religious obligations to the people but also by working in the areas of education and enlightenment. From the time of their arrival the Basilians began publishing Ukrainian-language newspapers, established Ukrainian cultural, enlightenment and athletic societies, theatre groups and choirs, and were instrumental in the formation of Ukrainian schools. Assisting them in their work was the Order of the Sisters Servants (Sestry Sluzhebnytsi) which continues to function alongside the Basilians in their important roles as teachers and educators.

Even with the difficulties in adapting to their new life in Brazil, the settlers did not wallow in misery but worked hard to improve their fate. As always, it was the desire to provide something better for their children which sustained them. *Mozhe nam tam bude dobre, tilko tra pryterpity. Yak my dobra ne dizhdaiem, to bodai khoch nashi dity.* (Perhaps it will be good for us there, but it will take some getting used to. If we find no prosperity for ourselves, then at least for our children.) It was the Church which eased their transition as snakes, spiders and the sadness for the homeland could temporarily be forgotten through the comforts of prayer and worship. Settling and living together, with family members or among other Ukrainians, gave the people a sense of protection, strength and security and provided a favourable environment for identity retention, the effects of which in varying degrees have been in evidence since the first years in Brazil.

■ ■ ■

It is a beautiful October day here in Prudentópolis. As I write this, I am sitting on the Praça Ucrânia (Ukraine Square), the bronze statue of Taras Shevchenko at my left, the shiny cupolas of São Josafat's Ukrainian Catholic Church to my right and from across the street I can hear two women speaking in Ukrainian about the price of potatoes. More than a century after the arrival of the first Ukrainians in Brazil—sitting in the very spot from which many of them set out to begin their new lives—I cannot help but feel the ghosts all around me.

The Ukrainian immigration continues to maintain a prominent presence in the Brazilian South, particularly in the state of Paraná where the colonization was at its strongest. As in Prudentópolis and its environs, with 77 percent of the population tracing its origins to a Ukrainian immigrant ancestor, the evidence is everywhere. Houses, surrounded by fruit trees, flower gardens and fences are typically based on old-country models and painted in the traditional colours of white, blue and green. Ukrainian Catholic churches, built in the Byzantine style and found throughout the whole of the municipality, serve the community's faithful. Ukrainian, for many the language of choice over Portuguese, is widely spoken among all age groups. If it were not for the palms, the Paraná pine trees and the red soil, this could be almost any town in Western Ukraine.

No less impressive is the Ukrainian contribution to the socio-economic development of the region. Lifetimes of hard work and determination turned vast stretches of untouched forest into fields of arable land which are still under cultivation today. European crops, such as buckwheat and mint, have been successfully introduced by the immigrants. Their work on road building, performed initially in order to pay off land debts, produced an extensive transportation network where only trails and paths had previously existed. As the colonies became established, so did schools, hospitals, orphanages, stores and National Homes (types of community halls), all at their own initiative and expense The Ukrainian settlement in Paraná, Santa Catarina and Rio Grande do Sul, and indeed that of other immigrant groups living alongside, has given the South a distinct cultural character not found in any other parts of the country.

A few days have passed and I am in the nearby colony of Cônsul Pohl. This was the home of my immigrant ancestor and I have travelled in the company of family and friends to see where he lived. The settlement is fairly typical of those from the first wave of immigration; that is, a *linha* or line village consisting of rectangular lots running back at right angles on both sides of a trail or road. A Ukrainian school was established as early as 1911. Church was attended in neighbouring Nova Galícia. Grounds were donated for a cemetery so that burials could take place locally. Other families from the same village in Galicia emigrated and settled alongside.

"My grandfather used to say that the angels had forgotten him and his family," my cousin tells me. "They set out across the ocean, leaving the only home they ever knew in order to make a better life for themselves. They were overwhelmed by difficulties, despair and loneliness. It took them six months, using an axe and a saw shared among six families, to cut down one pinheiro. Men and women carried timbers on their backs in great distances for the building of houses and churches. In the same week they celebrated the birth of one child and mourned the loss of another. Their lives were full of hard work and self-sacrifice, the likes of which our generation will never know. If only they could come back for one day to see that it had not been in vain."

Built on the foundations which were laid by the first arrivals, the Ukrainian community in Brazil has presently grown to nearly a 500,000 people, the majority still confined to the country's southern regions. Within, ethnic identity, the ancestral language, culture and religion have been retained to a respectable degree despite the assimilatory influences of the Brazilian environment. It is a legacy which is perpetuated and celebrated by the now third, fourth and even fifth-generation descendants of the pioneers but it has come at a price. The same factors which fostered identity retention-most significantly the nature of their settlement and the slow move towards urbanization-have kept the community relatively impoverished, poorly integrated into the regional economy and beyond the mainstream of Brazilian society. Despite the difficulties, and after all the changes and adaptations to life in the New World, at its essence remains the undeniable and unbreakable Ukrainian spirit. The pioneers would be pleased.

Chapter 1: About Free Lands

Dr. Yosyf Oleskiv

> Yosyf (also Osyp) Oleskiv was born on September 28, 1860 in the village of Skvariava Nova, county Zhovkva, East Galicia. An educator, agronomist, social activist and prominent member of the burgeoning Lviv intelligentsia, Oleskiv played a decisive role in the emigration of Ukrainians to the Americas at the turn of the last century. It was the small but growing number of Ukrainians having already left for Brazil as early as 1891 and their ensuing and disturbing reports of the conditions of settlement which prompted him to try to direct the emigration elsewhere.
>
> Working quickly, Oleskiv researched and wrote a booklet entitled *Pro vilni zemli (About Free Lands)* in which he described Canada as a more suitable place for Ukrainian settlement than Brazil. It was published by Lviv's Prosvita Society in 1895 and distributed throughout Galicia. The information it contained was largely responsible for reducing the number of Ukrainian emigrants to Brazil and redirecting their migration to Canada. Oleskiv died in 1903, not seeing the full results of his work but leaving a lasting legacy in the form of the first Ukrainian settlements in Canada.
>
> The following excerpt from *Pro vilni zemli* is Oleskiv's discussion about Brazil.

If someone asked me to describe in one word what Brazil means for our emigrants, that word would be grave. Not only a grave for their hopes for a better future but also a grave in its most literal sense. I am certain that everyone, in following and weighing carefully the facts as I give them here word for word, will come to this same conclusion.

How was it that the people heard about Brazil and began to emigrate there? In order to understand, we must go to Brazil itself, a country which lies on the other side of the world and where, as has already been said, Christmas is in summer and the harvest in winter. Brazil is a very large country, the same size as all of Europe. The climate is hot. Most parts of Brazil are covered with impenetrable forests through which you have to cut a path step-by-step with an axe. The land is swampy and muddy, the ground baked in the eternal heat which produces a volatile smell from the rotting animal and vegetable remains. The yellow fever epidemic, so deadly in the low-lying areas and at the coast, will never be eradicated and claims numerous lives year after year. Only the mountains and highlands are free from this disease. Mandioca (1), coffee and cotton are cultivated in the provinces of Paraná and Santa Catarina, both of which lie further south where the climate is more temperate (everything there is in reverse) as in southern Italy. It is possible for our grains, especially corn, to be cultivated in Paraná. They are experimenting with rye but it appears that the weather is too hot because the grain withers and looks as if it were burned.

Brazil's main crops are sugar cane, coffee and cotton, the cultivation of which requires a great deal of work and effort through the whole year. The Brazilians were engaged in the African slave trade up until 1888. These slaves, who were whipped, tortured, shackled, neglected and even beaten to death for the smallest disobedience, worked for their masters on the coffee and cotton plantations. Slavery was abolished in Brazil by a decree of the Brazilian Emperor on May 13, 1888, on which day 800,000 Africans became free people. In their first expression of freedom, they abandoned the miserable prisons where they had been so brutally treated and escaped into the forests.

Гей! розіллялось ти, руськеє горе,
Геть по Європі і геть поза море!

Yosyf Oleskiv

At first, they were reluctant to accept any paying jobs on the plantations and in no way wanted to return to their former prisons. The plantations stood empty, they became overgrown and the owners were barely able to keep the smallest part in operation because of the lack of labourers. The Brazilians were enraged. In their anger they removed their Emperor from the throne but it did not help. It was necessary at all costs to acquire workers for the plantations. In order to recruit people to Brazil, the government dispatched paid agents throughout Europe, mainly among the Poles and Ruthenians, and began to transport the emigrants at its own expense.

On one hand, there was the utter poverty of the homeland which removed all possibility for a productive life. On the other hand, the agents spread their wild and wonderful news about the Brazilian wealth and free passage across the sea, all of which fanned the flames of emigration fever. There is hope that these flames will soon become extinguished as some of the first Brazilian casualties, those who lost their last *kreuzer* (2), their families and their health, start to return home. There will be more and more of these people returning and bringing with them the truth about life in Brazil.

Thousands of Poles and Ruthenians are stranded in Brazilian ports, wandering, waiting and wanting to return to Galicia but there is no one willing to send them back for free. A return trip costs several hundred *zoloti rynski* and so many people use the last of their strength and energy to try and earn some money to get home. The whole of this emigration will eventually return to Galicia but in numbers ten times less than those who left. The rest will be lying in Brazilian graves.

Brazil directed the emigrants to work on coffee and cotton plantations but our people hoped to get their own land and they wanted to settle in the colonies, especially in the provinces of Paraná, Santa Catarina and Rio Grande do Sul where the climate is more temperate and where they could adapt. In seeing this, the government closed the provinces [to settlement] and no longer allowed the people to go to the colonies in order to force them to work on the plantations. (3) The officials said that the colonists had staged a protest and so they would not send any more people there. At the same time the Brazilian government reduced the number of free tickets to 500 monthly which they gave to the St. Raphael Society for distribution.

Бачили мури Любляни і Р'єки,
Як з свого краю біг русин навтеки.

The aim of the St. Raphael Society, and also that of its Galician affiliate, is to curb the emigration and protect the welfare of the emigrants (4). Mr. Henryk Wielowiejski, a landowner from Pokuttia, and Count Potolicki are actively involved in this Society. This consists of transporting the emigrants from Lviv to Italy in such a way that they do not spend more on that trip than is necessary and obtaining a Polish lawyer to provide assistance for the emigrants in Genoa or Udine. It is in these cities that the people are most vulnerable, losing the last of their money through ignorance or at the hands of dishonest agents.

With that ends the assistance which is provided to the emigrants. The only further advice they receive is that under no circumstances should they allow themselves to be sent to the plantations in other provinces. The only exception to this is the state of São Paulo, which borders Paraná, and then only so that one day they might resettle in Paraná if the government reopens the area for colonization. A Polish priest is supposed to be available in the port city of Santos in the state of São Paulo in order to provide advice for the emigrants and to assist them in finding work. In practise this provides little results because the priest is still unfamiliar with Brazil and settlement there.

The fact, then, is that people are being sought for labourers in Brazil, nothing more. Try to imagine something more undesirable or unproductive than this. A dark cloud of agents descends upon the emigrants on their arrival at the Brazilian ports and takes them to work on plantations, sometimes more than 100 miles inland. Workers are usually contracted for a period of three years such that it is impossible to ever leave. They are billed for food and other provisions which keep them forever in debt. The arrangement is not much different from slavery. Our people even lived in the former slave lock-ups where the shackles still lie in the corners.

The front facade of the former Immigration Hostelry in São Paulo, now the Museu da Imigração, 1937.

For several years, a Jew was contracting Hutsuls (5) to work for a man in Romania. The man, in believing that the Hutsuls would not find any justice beyond the border, exploited them terribly, so much so that they escaped during the night and crossed the border back to Galicia. Romania borders our country and so they were able to escape. But what will the Poles and Ruthenians do, exploited and treated like slaves in these plantations deep in Brazil? To whom can they complain? Where can they flee? They will find no justice in the government because the officials always take the side of their own, the landowners...

It is enough that the poor farmer will experience a bitter fate there —but if you want to go to Hell while still living in this lifetime, then go to Brazil!

Land parcels are no longer given out free in Brazil. Before Paraná was closed to settlement, emigrants were given 20-hectares of forest, not for free but for a payment of 250 *rynski* to which nine percent interest was added. In addition, everything he ate from the time that he arrived on his land to the first harvest was

Руські зітхання і стогнання лунали
Там де Понтеби біліють скали.

recorded on account. This led to great expenses. By the time our colonist had his first bowl of *kulesha* (6), he was so debt-ridden that he would never be free.

And that first harvest was such a long way off! The officials, who receive money for the keeping of the emigrants, detain several hundred people in the barracks for months on end, sometimes even a half-year, before they are able to settle on their land. The people were so anxious to begin work but the officials did not even think about letting them go. During that time their debts grow because every little crumb is recorded on their account. Finally they are sent to the colonies. This is forest with neither a city nor a village for several miles around. Wild Botocudos (7) attack and kill the colonists from time to time. The forest is so large that an axe hardly makes a dent as the 20-hectare parcels are measured out for the immigrant. Fire is needed to assist in the clearing. You could clear ten *morgs* (8) of our forest in the time it takes to clear one *morg* here.

Finally, a small piece of field is cleared, worked with a hoe and planted with a little seed corn. There is hope. But do not be too happy because after working for several years as the farmer clears himself a couple *morgs* for cultivation, he starts to farm and begins to pay off his debts for the land and provisions. But where will he get a *kreuzer*? He cannot work at a job because there are none. This is forest. There are no larger cities around except for Curitiba and it is located several miles from the newest colonies. The whole country is separated from the sea by a chain of mountains covered with impassable Brazilian forest. There is only one train for transporting grain for sale and export from the colonies to the coast but the shipping costs are prohibitively high. There are no transportation routes. The people need every *kreuzer* to pay off their debts and to purchase provisions for the house or farm. There are no factories in Paraná and everything is imported from afar. Duty raises the prices of goods so much that those which are destined for the colonies cost four times more than in Galicia. Whereas we would pay 40 to 50 *kreuzer* for a simple axe, it costs 3,800 *mil reis* (9) in Brazil which converts to approximately four *zoloti rynski*.

There were some immigrants in Paraná who were smarter than the Ruthenians and Poles, some 6,000 Germans who settled there in the years 1873-74 but soon left. They went on to Argentina where they found good land and are living and farming very well.

A newspaper advertisement (in Polish) offering travel services for emigrants to Brazil. The next transport, it informs, would be leaving Lviv at the beginning of May 1896 and departing from Bremen, Germany, for the port of Paranaguá, Paraná on the 10th of the month. Prospective emigrants were to call at the Hotel George in Lviv.

Аж із Кормон, мов живого до гробу,
Гнали жандарми наш люд, як худобу.

I say once again that the Brazilian government is no longer allowing settlement on the colonies but is taking people for work on the plantations.

The saddest part of the emigration to Brazil is the loss of life or health. The voyage from the shores of Italy to those of Brazil, lasting three weeks, is marked with bitter suffering. It is a bloody road. Seasickness, and the violent vomiting it causes, affects those who have never travelled by sea and spares no one. It would not be so bad if it were just you alone. But imagine several hundred people, all packed in one room below the deck like herrings in a barrel, where the beds are stacked one on top of another with barely enough room to walk between them, becoming seasick at the same time. Imagine further the three weeks of travel with such unbearable heat as the ship crosses the equator, the repugnant stench of this human sty, the terrible stuffiness and the disgusting filth. No one could remain healthy in such conditions. Everyone was sallow and weak with children and the infirm succumbing.

Ultimately the emigrants arrive in Rio de Janeiro, Brazil's capital city. A hotel was built for the emigrants, on an island located a distance from the city, where they would stay until being sent to their appointed destination. The emigrants were treated well and adjusted to their accommodations. The following descriptions are from the book by Messrs. Hempel and Siemyradzki who travelled to Brazil in order to observe the plight of the emigrants... (10)

The Portal do Imigrante, located at the entrance to Prudentópolis, built in commemoration of the city's centennial of Ukrainian settlement in 1995.

Mr. Hempel writes in his travel notes: "When the newly arrived immigrants began dying of yellow fever in April of last year in the unhealthy port city of Rio de Janeiro, they were sent to Pinheiro, a town in the mountains which was safe from the disease."

We learn more about Pinheiro from Hempel: "Almost all of the young children have died. A hundred within a month. In spite of the eternally rampant yellow fever, the capital of Rio de Janeiro is regarded as a place of salvation and, for those who escaped here from the coffee plantations, it truly is salvation. Many people are sick and dying... All day long Negroes stumble up and down the streets, carrying coffins on their heads as they transport bodies to the cemetery. Of all the immigrants who are left in Rio de Janeiro, the majority is dying or going elsewhere..."

The emigrants' accommodations in the city of São Paulo are completely different from those in Rio de Janeiro. "From the entranceway, an intolerable stench wafts throughout. Stuffiness, dirt and a repugnant smell remind one of the voyage on board the ship. Several immigrant women, their husbands lying in the hospitals, are huddled in the corner of one room. Two newly arrived families sit in another. Barely two days in Brazil, they are already not feeling well. They are unable to eat the food, just dried meat and stinking fish, which is provided here. They are overcome by despair, surrounded by so many sick children, without money and in a foreign land!"

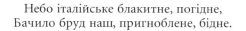

Небо італійське блакитне, погідне,
Бачило бруд наш, пригноблене, бідне.

The accommodations in Santos: "The place is full of dirt. The stench is unbearable. It is even worse than in São Paulo. Everyone complains of the climate here which, in this nest of yellow fever, is deadly. The immigrants curse Brazil and those who praised its virtues. Our people cannot believe it when they see a dog or someone with a cigar in church. This is normal. Clearly, God is nowhere to be found here, they say."

The accommodations are even worse in Paraná, in Curitiba. "All of the immigrants sit on the floor and the women, through tears, show us the thin and tattered mats on which they had to sleep amidst the filth and vermin. Some spend between three and six months waiting for their land; you almost never see young children here. The worst is the third emigration home where 940 emigrants sleep together in bunk beds stacked like on the ship! The conditions are terrible. The sick are lying amongst the healthy, mothers give birth next to those who are dying. Four to five corpses are carried out daily.

The colonies along Paraná's Iguaçu River: "The mortality here in the colonies is considerable. Thirty people died in Rio dos Patos between March and September, a period of half-a-year. More than a tenth of the immigrants in the colonies of Paraná have died within a year. Twenty to 25 percent of the immigrants in the barracks and in the colonies have died. What will be happening next? The colonies will not be able to grow and develop as a result of the high mortality rates."

Rio Negro. From Hempel and his companion's series of descriptions of the terrible conditions in the colonies in the Rio Negro area, the following is about the colony of São Pedro: "A simple line extends through the eternal forest, a narrow path with the trees cleared only as much as to make a little path (eventually this will be a road because the farmsteads of the colonists are located in the forest on both sides). Two little huts stand on the right side of the path. These are the homes of the colonists. Covered with some old rags and lying unconscious in front of one of them is a young man suffering from typhus. He is Jaworski from Warsaw, a labourer at Sperling factory. A young woman with her little son in her arms cries as she sits beside him. Inside the hut they have nothing more than some black beans. It is 46 kilometres from here to the nearest store for provisions.

An old woman and her daughter sit in the other hut. Both of them were ill and are just now returning to health. A teenaged boy lies beside the hut with his stomach swollen like a mountain. The women are so weak they are barely able to speak. We ask for their husbands. 'He went to Rio Negro for supplies a couple of days ago but has still not returned. Hempel and Siemyradzki found 1,952 immigrants in the barracks in Rio Negro. They were weak from starvation, exploited by the officials, tormented by fever, typhus and dying like flies. We went to the cemetery in order to see exactly how many lives have been claimed by Brazil. The grave digger, a German, showed us 134 graves of our emigrants, all newly dug in the last few months when the 'colonization' of the cemetery began. In reality, more corpses lie in the cemetery than there are people living in the colonies..."

This is the Hell of life in Paraná. I repeat that the government has continued to close settlement in the colonies and is only sending people to work on the coffee plantations in conditions which are even worse than those in the colonies...

Генуя довго мабуть не забуде,
Як то гостили в гій руські люди.

Chapter 2 | ABOUT EMIGRATION
Dr. Yosyf Oleskiv

> **About Emigration (O emigratsii),** Oleskiv's second booklet, was published in Lviv in 1895 upon his return to Galicia from a visit to Canada and the United States. It reaffirmed his earlier position that the only viable option for Ukrainian settlement was in Canada, not Brazil, and placed the blame squarely on the shoulders of the unscrupulous steamship company agents who lured the peasants under pretense and false promise to Brazil. "Our people go around asking for advice from everyone," he wrote, "until they meet up with some little Jew or an agent who paints for them a picture of a paradise across the sea in Brazil where trained monkeys work for the people." There was no Brazilian paradise, he added, and while he maintained that Canada was a hundred times better than Brazil, he cautioned that there would be difficulties there too.
>
> Oleskiv presented the settlement options in the form of a comparison between Brazil and Canada as follows:

Their misery driving them to panic and confusion, the people are selling off their land no longer for half the price but for a third or even a quarter of its value in order to gain at least the hope of getting to that Paraná in Brazil where, they say, you can not only get land for free but a monkey as well which would work the field while the peasant enjoys a well-deserved rest on top of the clay oven (1).

It is a completely futile effort to talk sense to such people who believe in monkeys as labourers and that our archdukes and duchesses are coaxing them to Brazil. What does a stupid man care about sense? A stupid head is only full of stupid things.

That which I am writing here is designed for more sensible people and which will perhaps prove useful for those living in this country or another.

In the latter part of July of this year I travelled to America together with one of our peasants (intelligent by our Galician standards) in order to determine if there is free land of good quality and whether or not our people would be able to find a better life there. Another peasant had planned to travel with me but was unable to obtain the money necessary for the trip and so he stayed behind. We spent the whole summer travelling, covering some 10,000 English miles in America (the English mile is less, about a quarter of one of our miles). The length of the railroad alone from one end of Canada to the other is over 3,000 English miles. With such distances, these are the things to deal with there. Every American country is as big as the whole world in which we live, namely Europe. The United States is the same size as Europe, Canada is just as big and so is Brazil. Our peasants cannot even learn the name of the country. They pronounce Brazil as Bryzolia or Brenzolia and for Paraná (the name of one of the Brazilian provinces) they say Parania (2). They think that travelling to Brazil is no more of an adventure than going to a village some five or six miles away! And yet one such word like Brazil or Canada means so much more! (3)

It would be possible to travel by the fastest express train for whole days across nearly barren rocks, through eternal forests and thickly overgrown swamps, through arid deserts where crops could never be cultivated and across such wide and steep hills and not even see a place where you could build a house...

 Будуть ще внукам казати проти ночі—
«Дивний тут люд кочував із півночі.

A letter from Silvio Nodari to Ivan Vovna of the village of Ivanivka, Skalat county, confirming third-class steamship passage for him and his family to Brazil. Nodari's reservations were made with the company Ligure Brasiliana, departing from Genoa on December 4, 1895. The passengers were required to be in Pontebba (by rail through Vienna, Loben and Pontafel) on November 30.

There are, however, places in the United States, Canada, Argentina, Siberia and in many other countries–only not in Paraná or in Brazil as a whole—where you will find great expanses of unoccupied rich black soil waiting to be ploughed and which is being given out for free or for only a few gulden (4) per *morg*!

A COMPARISON BETWEEN BRAZIL AND OTHER COUNTRIES (UNITED STATES AND CANADA)

In Brazil an immigrant receives 20 *morgs* of virgin forest on credit for a price of up to 500 *zoloti rynski*. The rate of interest is 20 *zoloti rynski* per year. (As can be seen, the Brazilian government created such conditions for the immigrants who were so determined to settle on land of their own. This way, they will go bankrupt after several years, they will have to leave the land and eventually go to those places for which they were actually brought in; that is, for work on the coffee plantations of the Brazilian landlords, in place of slaves...) (5)

In Brazil the forest is so thick that an entire year of work is required to clear no more than a *morg*. Therefore, for one *morg* of field, the immigrant pays not only with money but with a whole year of work which everywhere in America, and also the same in Brazil, is worth several hundred *zoloti rynski*.

The Brazilian forests, where our people are settling, are located 15 to 20 miles from the closest railroad. The country is completely wild, there is nowhere to sell the grain, there is no kind of industry (for a useless axe you have to pay four *zoloti rynski*) and there are no ways to earn money. In addition, the Brazilian currency is worth very little and everything is double in price. Taxes are high.

The climate in Brazil, even in Paraná, is unsuitable for our people because apart from yellow fever which also occurs here, everyone goes through a period of the so-called acclimatization disease.

The trip to Brazil, to the farmstead itself, travelling without stop, takes approximately a month-and-a-half. Still in Europe, our people wait for weeks for the steamship in Udine or, as it is now, months while being fleeced of their last *kreuzer* by the bloodsucking agents (6). In Paraná, the immigrants are kept for months in the barracks at their own cost before being taken to their land.

«Рідну країну з слізми споминав він,
Але з прокляттям із неї втікав він.

The journey to Brazil goes through a [so-called] hot belt and people, especially the children, die from the heat along the way. Newspapers report how our women jump into the water after the corpses of their children who have died.

The most important item is the steamship ticket to Brazil which was previously given out free of charge. Presently agent Nodari, from whom the St. Raphael Society obtained tickets, wrote to Lviv telling that the transports are being stopped for seven months and each person who sent him a deposit will be refunded upon request. The reason for this is that Italian authorities are investigating Nodari for fraud against the Galician emigrants. Many who obtained free passage for themselves ended up paying more for it than if they had bought a ticket to the United States or Canada (7).

In Canada and in certain places in the United States, the emigrant receives 113 *morgs* of free land, paying only 25 *zoloti rynski* for the cost of surveying.

In Canada, the United States, Argentina and Siberia, the land is of the highest quality (black prairie soil) and ready for the plough. Apart from the free land, you can purchase additional land for less than ten *zoloti rynski* and that of the highest quality, located near the railroad and near the cities, for 25 *zoloti rynski*. In view of that, what can we think about the integrity or about the information of those people who are enticing our villagers to Brazil?! In Canada, the United States and Argentina, it is possible to purchase land near the railroad for a few *zoloti rynski* per *morg*.

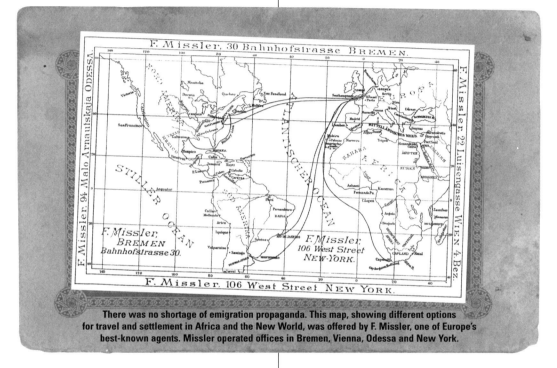

There was no shortage of emigration propaganda. This map, showing different options for travel and settlement in Africa and the New World, was offered by F. Missler, one of Europe's best-known agents. Missler operated offices in Bremen, Vienna, Odessa and New York.

The information which I provided about the unsuitability of Brazil does not apply to these countries. In the United States, Canada, Argentina, Russia and even Siberia the climate, though more severe in places, is invariably healthy. The same fruits we grow here can also be cultivated there.

The journey right to the place of settlement in Canada or the United States takes about two weeks. The ship travels through a belt of moderate climate and the voyage across the sea does not create a higher mortality.

The cost of the trip to the place of settlement in Canada is about 120 *zoloti rynski* per person. It is necessary to have the same amount of money when travelling to the United States, specifically to those areas where our people are going to work. Although the passage is less expensive, the immigrants are expected to have 40 *zoloti rynski* on hand or otherwise risk being sent back to Europe.

What can we conclude from this comparison? Is there no other answer than: go to the United States or to Canada, take the land which is being given free of charge or sold on credit for little money and begin farming?

I thought so too before my trip to America but my opinions have changed on one point. I was not disappointed in Canada or the United States, because there I found everything as it should be, but I was disappointed in our people.

 «Спродував дома поля, господарство,
Вірячи байці про Рудольфа царство.

The house (background) and field of a Ukrainian family in Brazil.

«Дома покинувши землю родинну,
Гнався, щоб мрію ловити дитину.

Chapter 3: The First to Arrive

João Pacevicz

> João Pacevicz (Ivan Pasevych) was among the first Ukrainians to arrive in Brazil, settling near Mallet in the colony of Rio Claro, Paraná, in 1891. His story was published in *Prácia* on December 12, 1951. He was concerned that more stories of the immigrants and their experiences in Brazil be recorded for posterity. These people, he said, were, "living testimonies to the settlement of the Brazilian South" and that with each of their deaths valuable sources of information were being lost.

It was May 1891. My family and I bid farewell to our native village of Servyriv, county Zolochiv, as we left for far-off Brazil in search of a new home. I was 15. We travelled with four other families. There was me, my parents Fedir and Sofia and my sisters Maryna, Hannia and Yustyna. We were separated from the others after our arrival in Paranaguá and would never see them again (1).

We travelled to the port of Hamburg, Germany, at our own cost and then from there to Rio de Janeiro at the expense of the state (2). We boarded the ship on July 6 and arrived in Rio on August 23. There were problems in Brazil, a revolution between the Federalists and the Pica Pau, and so we waited for a long time in Africa and then in Rio before being allowed to disembark (3). We were transported by smaller boats from the ship to Ilha das Flores (4) where we waited for about six weeks. From the island, they took us by another ship further south to the port of Paranaguá and from there to Curitiba.

At that time the city of Curitiba was very small. And it was full of mud puddles. The streets were narrow and you would often get stuck in the mud where Rio Branco Street is today. The train from Paranaguá went no further than Curitiba. We were put up in barracks—just outside of the city centre where Sete de Setembro Street is presently located—where we stayed for three months.

My father went out to work, earning about two-and-a-half *mil reis* (5) a day, while we stayed at the barracks with mother. Our time spent in Curitiba was longer than we expected because the road to Porto Amazonas was still being built. When it was completed, we were loaded onto *carroças* (6) and taken to Porto Amazonas, travelling along the Iguaçu River. Our journey lasted six days. Arriving in Barra Feia, we were given accommodations in little huts made of bamboo. The road to the colony of Rio Claro was still being built and so we walked for two weeks, our baggage piled high on the backs of mules, before reaching the settlement. We stayed here for a couple of months, living in bamboo huts while the *shakry* (7) were being surveyed.

With the formalities completed, my father claimed *shakra* Number 64. Collecting our possessions and carrying everything on our backs, we walked to Rio Claro where we saw a larger hut, also made of bamboo, which would serve as our house. Father had received a *foice* (8) and an axe and so he began at once to clear a piece of land nearby. We later began cutting through and clearing some of the forest so that we would be able to plant some kind of a crop.

The forest was deep and dark and full of snakes and wild animals. They would come right up to the house and they frightened us, especially since it was difficult to chase them away. Having cleared some land, my father sowed five litres of rye by

«Смілий у мріях, у вірі безглядний,
В дійсности наче дитина безрадний.

hand. The land had never been cultivated before and so it produced a good first harvest, about 96 quarts (9) from those five litres of seed. Father made a grist mill and we ground some flour. I can still taste the bread today. It was the same kind we ate in Galicia.

It was difficult settling here because we lived among Polish immigrants for the first three years. Afterwards the first Ukrainians came to settle in Rio Claro, eight families by the names of Povidaiko, Sheremeta, Bilenky, Pashko, Kozhan, Kraskovsky, Marushka and Yustyshyn. As soon as we found out about their arrival, we went to greet them with [the traditional offering of] bread. By this time we had already begun farming, we cleared some cropland, we had some grain and we owned a cow which was bought with the money I had earned (a cow and two calves for 60 *mil reis*).

There was no church here when we arrived. Holy days like Christmas and Easter were celebrated at home. I remember Father blessed the *paska* (10) with holy water and we recited "Our Father." This was how we celebrated. The first church was built in 1897. It was located a good distance away and so we would travel there by foot, two or three times a year, a walk which took us a couple of days. The people began to build a church in Serra de Tigre in 1899. Father and I helped to cut the timber for the framing, carrying the logs on our shoulders from the forest to the building site. Even Father Rozdolsky (11) helped in the construction. Many were involved. From foundation to shingles, the required materials were transported on the backs of the people. The church was completed in 1900.

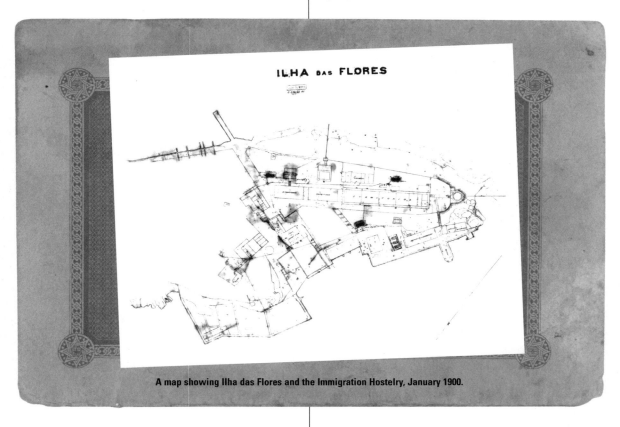

A map showing Ilha das Flores and the Immigration Hostelry, January 1900.

There were more and better roads by this time and so it was easier for the people to travel to church. The railroad had still not reached these parts. The colonies of Dorizon and Mallet were yet to be carved out of the dark forest. The rail line from Curitiba to Ponta Grossa, and from there to Porto União, was begun in 1892. The road to Mallet was built in 1907 and then to Porto União in 1908. There were no schools and no teachers. Those who were literate taught the others. The first school was built in Serra de Tigre in 1905. The teacher was Mykola Futerko. The Mohyla Society also existed there and did very well. It dissolved, unfortunately, after the death of Father Rozdolsky. The Ukrainian newspaper *Zoria* was founded in Curitiba in 1907. Yearly subscription rates, as I remember, were seven *mil reis*.

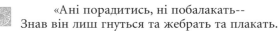

«Ані порадитись, ні побалакать--
Знав він лиш гнуться та жебрать та плакать.

And so the years passed. With the railroad station located close by, Dorizon began to grow. A schoolhouse was built in 1910 and named in honour of Taras Shevchenko. The teacher was Mr. Kuts, an immigrant from the old country who arrived in Brazil in 1911. The settlers also established a Ukrainian Society of Taras Shevchenko. The most active in the community was Mr. Antin Firman in whose home many of the events and celebrations took place. The first Congress of Ukrainians in Brazil was held in Dorizon in 1912.

Now after 60 years of life here in Brazil, everything that we lived through and experienced seems like a dream. In this dream I see the dark forest, the charred stumps and the narrow paths of the first years of settlement. The old people have died and have left this place for the youth. It is sad that our young people have forgotten about the sacrifices and hardships of our first years in Brazil. All that is here today is because of the sweat—and at times blood—of the pioneers.

Ukrainians clearing the forest (*foisuvannia*).

Гей, розіллялось ти, руськеє горе,
Геть по Європі і геть поза море!

Ukrainian men and women working on the building of the roads near Prudentópolis.

Доки Гамбурзькі, важкі паровози—
Де ви не ллялися руськії сльози!

Chapter 4: Our Beginnings in Rio Claro

Teodoro Potoskei

> Potoskei's group was the first to settle in the colony of Rio Claro, Paraná in 1895. His account of the early years of settlement was published in *Svoboda*, North America's first Ukrainian daily, in 1898. He was later asked to write about Ukrainian life in Brazil for the newspaper on a regular basis. Potoskei was very proud of his colony's accomplishments in such a short period of time—church, school and reading club all within the first two years of settlement. "Imagine the difficulties for such poor immigrants," he wrote. "So many obstacles and challenges and yet we were able to overcome..." Potoskei's account, as follows, was written in Rio Claro in September 1897.

It is with great pleasure that I am writing to you today. We are all so pleased that you are sending us *Svoboda*. Everyone reads it or they come and listen [to it being read aloud] at our reading club which was founded here in Rio Claro on July 25, 1897. It is located next to the church in the house which we built for our priest, Father N. Rozdolsky (1). It cost us 1,000 *mil reis* to build. The school is located there too. We have 40 students and more and more are attending everyday. So far we have only been able to finish Father Rozdolsky's lodgings because we have run out of money. The schoolroom still needs painting. Things are so difficult here. Even if we had something which we could sell, our colony is located so far away from the others. The only way to earn money is to go out and work in another colony or for the Brazilians on their herba (2) plantations. Sometimes the Poles from the town of Rio Claro will come and buy beans, corn, rye or buckwheat but the money from these sales is only enough for some salt or oil for the lamps. Nothing more.

We meet at the reading club after church on Sundays. The children attend school everyday with the lessons finishing at noon. We still do not have a teacher because we have no money to pay a proper salary but God has given us a priest who teaches our children without asking for anything in return. He sees our limitations here. It has been a difficult two years since we arrived.

When we came here, the forests and hills were such that you could not even find a place to set down your foot. But we are a colony now—a village, even—with wooden houses lining both sides of the road and our Ruthenian (3) church standing on a hill in the very centre of the settlement. There is no other Ruthenian church in the whole of Brazil which is as beautiful as ours. Our Ruthenian pride and glory is alive and well here! The bell tower and the house for the priest, reading club and school are located beside.

The Poles have been settled in the neighbouring colony of Rio Claro for seven years already but they still do not have a church of their own, just a little chapel which is no grander than any one of our poor little Ruthenian houses. They attend our services because their closest priest is in Curitiba. If God wills, we are planning to build a new church in the next couple of years. We can do this if we all stick together but there are some Ruthenians who within a week are, as we say, "one day Ruthenian but six days Polish." They do not support the church or the reading club but, thankfully, their numbers are few. Their complaints about the priest are unfounded and it is not true that Father Rozdolsky exploits the people. He takes very little from us because he knows how difficult the beginnings are for the colonist. He encourages the people to remain united and not to abandon their

 Всі з тебе, Русине, рвали проценти,
Польські шляхтичі і швабські агенти.

I chervona nyva bilyi khlib vrodyla. (Even a field of red soil produces white bread.) Harvest time, Ukrainian settlers near Prudentópolis.

Що то ще жде тебе на океані?
Що у Бразилії, в славній Парані?

native language nor their faith. He teaches the children very well, providing lessons not only in Ruthenian but also in mathematics and Portuguese because we know that it is necessary to learn Brazil's language in addition to our own.

The Brazilians are very good with our people and they always come to our church. This is another reason why we need to be able to speak with them. They see how our people are working on the *shakry* (4) and they are impressed and want to do the same. Those Brazilians who live close by are following our example and are planting rye and potatoes and have learned to speak Ruthenian. Our people have been friendly with the Brazilians since we arrived here. We gave them bread which they did not want to accept at first because they did not know what it was. The Brazilians have not forgotten this and they have come to like our people, saying "Galician Ruthenians are good people" but the Poles, they are "not so good."

You asked me about our settlement here in Rio Claro. I arrived [in Brazil] from the village of Myshkaliv near Lviv on the first Saturday after Easter 1895. We were one of five families travelling together. There was me, my wife, my children Marta and Danylo and my sister Maria. I only had 100 *zoloti rynski* for the voyage. I still did not have complete ownership of my land and my father forbade me to sell it. I sold off my wife's field for 70 *zoloti rynski* and the other 30 came from my savings. I borrowed 100 from Tymko Barchyshyn who was also travelling with us. There were eight in Barchyshyn's family: he, his wife, two sons, two daughters, a son-in-law and his sister. Oleksa Narevach, his wife and two little children, came with 700 *zoloti rynski*. Vasyl Vozny, his wife and three children, had 300 *zoloti rynski*. My brother Vasyl Potoskei also made the trip with us. We spent seven weeks in Udine before getting a ship (5). Silvio Nodari was a thief who fleeced the people while they waited in Italy (6). I myself even paid him 62 *zoloti rynski*. But for what? We arrived in Genoa on June 6, 1895, boarded the steamship on June 8 and sailed for 22 days. The voyage was good, thanks to God, with no one suffering from seasickness or illness at all. Arriving in Paraná, we were taken into the forests to the colony of Rio Claro.

It is harvest time for us now (December 29, 1897). We have rye, barley, buckwheat and beans which God in His grace has made grow beautifully this year. Many crops are sown again after they are harvested. You can plant buckwheat three times a year here, barley and peas twice but rye only once. Everything grows very well. Wheat is not planted in great amounts because it is hard to protect the grain from the birds. Millet does very well, potatoes too which can be planted twice a year. No one plants oats because there is no need for it here.

You asked about our methods of farming. I can tell you that those who were hard-working peasants in Galicia are doing very well here in Brazil. Those who were lazy good-for-nothings at home have become Brazilian vagabonds. There are some people who do not look after their *shakry* or associate with the Brazilians. They earn, instead, a useless little amount of money and say that they will go back to Galicia because they cannot work on these forest-fields. It is true that there is a lot of work here. Even more so for a lazybones.

Around the end of September the people usually begin clearing a patch of land for a field. By the middle of October, the remaining underbrush is cleared out from between the larger trees and is left to dry for a week while the trees themselves are cut down. An area with large, thick-trunked trees offers the most fertile soil for the farmer but the work in clearing it is more difficult. Forests of *pin'ory* (7) and bamboo provide poorer soils but they are easier to clear. The trees are cut at their base with a sharp axe. It typically takes four or five men to cut and clear the same area of prime land that it would take only two men to clear a section of *pin'ory* or bamboo forest.

After they have been cut and left to dry in the sun for two to three weeks or a month, the next step is to burn off all of the trees, branches and stumps. A fire is lit and then you have to run away quickly because the ground practically shakes and hums from the heat of the fire as it burns. It is terrible to watch! When the fire has gone out and the ground cooled, you can then plant corn, beans, cucumbers, pumpkin, melons. This is how it is done: you take a stick, use it to make holes in the ground and throw in the seeds. The soil is so soft and light after the fire that you just want to walk barefoot through it. It needs no ploughing or digging. All you have to do is plant the seeds, cover them up with a hoe and then harvest corn, beans, rye, buckwheat, barley, peas, millet. The best fields and gardens are on these patches of burned forest. Vegetables, especially cabbage, beets, radishes, carrots, garlic and onions, do their very best if they are planted where the strongest part of the fire was. Flax grows very well but we still have not been able to grow hemp. It does poorly here. We have also had difficulties in getting beet seeds and have had to send for them from Galicia. Only a few of the people have cattle. The land here in our

The celebration of a holy day unites the faithful and their priest in common rejoice. Behind, a Ukrainian Catholic chapel and bell tower from the first years of settlement.

Сусіди любі! Пише вам Олеся.
Ми всі здорові і добре нам ведеться.

colony is good but it is not the same quality everywhere. In Jangada, for example, which is located 14 miles from here, the land is rocky and unproductive.

We would be so grateful if you could send us some seeds for growing fruit trees. We have none here in Rio Claro. There is a large orchard in Curitiba with all different types of European fruits but it has been difficult for us to get the seeds. We still have not planted any of our native fruits, only oranges and peaches. The peach is hard to describe. It is sort of like a Brazilian plum. I have some grape vines but they are still very young. I planted them only two years ago and grapes generally produce fruit in their third year.

Most of our people have planted grapes, oranges, sweet potatoes and these peaches. We also plant *mandioca* (8) whose tubers are used to make flour. They are dug, ground up and then you have *faryna*. It is very good to eat with meat or mixed into bread. They also grow bananas here in Paraná. Bananas are a type of fruit which looks like our Galician broad beans with long pods. If you remove the peel from these pods, it is just like butter inside, bright yellow and very sweet. We eat them spread on slices of bread. There is a tree here called *gavirato* which has very large, sweet berries similar to our Galician cherries. There is also a cherry tree with red-wine-coloured berries. Raspberries grow here as do blackberries. The berries from palms are not very good to eat. They are sweetish and tart at the same time. There are all kinds of forest trees but I only know the names of some of them: *pin'ory*, imbuia, saffron, cedar, camellia, palm, gavira and cherry. *Pin'ory*, imbuia and cedar provide the best wood for building. The air is clean here and the water is good. Everyone has bees and honey is produced in great amounts but there is no market for it because everyone has his own. We use only beeswax candles in church because those from paraffin are very expensive. Everyone has chickens but no one sells their eggs because there is no market.

A church brotherhood has been established for the colonists: that of St. Nykolai for the men and of the Holy Sacraments for the women. The young people are joining too. Membership costs 1,500 *mil reis* per year for men, 1,000 for women and one *mil reis* for the youth. Everyone is responsible for his own candles.

The Brazilians often attend our church. Those who live nearby want to belong to our Greek Catholic Church and our priest, Father Rozdolsky, has agreed to accept them if he receives permission from the Brazilian Bishop José in Curitiba. He is not certain if the Bishop will allow this. The Brazilians belong to the Roman Catholic Church and he fears that they will not adhere to our Eastern Rite. But they have seen that our churches, our services and our singing are more beautiful. They love all that is Ruthenian and they want to become a part. How could you not love our Ruthenian Rite? There is nothing more beautiful in the whole world!

Full of pride and promise, a group of settlers assembles for a photograph in front of their church.

Сім місяців отсе мовчали ми,
Аж на кінці мандрівки стали ми.

Our church was blessed on the fifth Sunday of Great Lent in 1897. Our priest, Father Rozdolsky, had a lot of trouble and many difficulties in getting it built. He lived with us for a few months, then later at Barchyshyn's, and we spent weeks discussing how we were going to do this. How would we begin to build a church when we did not even have ten *mil reis* of money? He said to me: "Well, Potoskei, what are we going to do?" I said: "We will build a church, and if it does not work out, then we will start over again."

The work took exactly 55 days to complete. Those who lived further off did not want to help with the construction but they changed their minds when they saw the cross on top of the cupola. I made the cross with my own hands. It was already Saturday evening and we wanted it to be in place for the blessing on Sunday. A lot of people had come to help—farmers and their wives, children, young men and women—but no one would go up on the roof to set it in place. So I climbed on top myself, they passed me the cross and I put it in place. Everyone sang *Mnohaya lita* (9). The church was ready for the blessing for the next day. It was a time of great celebration for us all. Everyone rejoiced because no one expected to see a Ruthenian church and hear Ruthenian singing so soon. Many from the colony had gone away to work and came home to see a church! When you heard the bells ring for the first time, your heart burst with joy. Even those with hearts of stone wept at our accomplishment.

There were many people involved in the building of the church. Those who worked the hardest were Hrynko Monchak, our glorious Ruthenian patriot, Mykhailo Maliuta, Tymko Barchyshyn, Vasyl Potoskei, Teodor Baran, Yosyf Hrytsiv, Ivan Ferynsovych [and] Dmytro Kobyletsky. Harasym Symbai, Vasyl Trach, Martyn and Ivan Rudatsky, Ilko Futerko and Oleksa Triska provided further assistance. The head carpenter was Panko Zavatsky from Barra Feia, 17 kilometres away. There were others involved but these men contributed the most.

The first Ukrainian Catholic church in Brazil, built in 1895, colonia Xavier da Silva, Santa Catarina.

The Poles, despite having been here longer, are still without their priest and are attending our church. Many of them speak Ruthenian but have retained their Polish faith. They see that our people are better off and that our priest exploits them less than their own. For example, our Ruthenian priest charges for services according to Brazilian practice: 13 *mil reis* for a marriage and three *mil reis* for a christening. Funerals cost six, eight or four *mil reis* but in most cases they are conducted free of charge.

In order to raise money for the church, it was decided that every *shakra* would donate 20 *mil reis* and ten *mil reis* from those living further away. Each *shakra* would also give two *mil reis* to the school and within a short time, 100 *mil reis* had been collected. It cost 2,800 *mil reis* to build the church and 1,000 to build the school. Messrs. Monchak, Maliuta, Ferynsovych, Symbai and others worked on the school. These debts give us no peace. We are so troubled. We would be grateful if you could advise us what to do. God is good. He will help. Somehow we will survive.

The air and water are good here in Rio Claro. I have not taken ill nor has anyone else. There is a large river, the Iguaçu, about two kilometres away. There are a lot of fish in it but no

Серед лісів живемо в бараці,
І маємо страшенно много праці.

one eats them because they have a very salty taste. It is a big river, big enough for a small steamship but there are rocks in so many places that a ship could never pass through. We go there to swim. Two mills are presently being built here. Dmytro Kovzhar is putting one up in our colony. He is the president of the church council, a successful farmer and owner of a *venda* (10) who settled here before we arrived. Andrukh Sobansky and his father-in-law Mr. Huchevsky are building a mill in the neighbouring colony. They will be in close proximity to the church and one another. We have our own Ruthenian smithy here (Hryhoriy Kulchytsky, a well-educated man), a shoemaker and tanner. The people are making great strides and are helping their own.

I can also tell you that our reading club is now serving as the colony's post office. When the priest and I went to Rio Claro for the mail, the postmaster gave us the letters for the whole colony which were then distributed from the reading club. One of the men agreed to go to town twice a month to pick up the mail and for this he will be paid 50 *mil reis* a year.

On behalf of all our Ruthenian colonists and members of the reading club, we thank you sincerely for the books, newspapers and calendars which you have sent us. We especially thank *Svoboda* for bringing us news from the homeland and from our American brothers. It comes here like a little Ruthenian swallow, comforting us as we cry bitterly and long for our native land, helping us as we start a new life in a new country.

We have learned so many lessons. Many immigrants were not able to cope and left Brazil or have become vagabonds. Those who came with some money and some possessions have been able to settle and adjust. Those who arrived without anything have found the transition difficult. So much money was wasted on the journey. The people ate, drank and enjoyed themselves because they were going to Brazil! To paradise! Where everything was free! To your health, my friend! But there was nothing when they came. No one gave them a house or an animal, just a large piece of forest 1,000 metres long and 250 metres wide and an axe, hoe, spade and foice to clear it. You have your land, now go to work!

The troubles were greater for those without any money. The people had their *shakra*, all forested, and began working to clear it. Together with their wife and children, they began cutting, planting and farming. Some went to work for the Brazilians on their herba plantations while others found jobs on the railroad. They earned some money, returned home to their families, bought some animals and worked on their land. It was their wives who looked after everything while they were away. God bless our Ruthenian women!

Ours is the best of all the Ruthenian colonies in Brazil and God has made this a very good year for us. We have enough of everything—except money. We still owe 1,500 *mil reis* on the church and we do not have the means to pay it. We will be able to earn some money if the railroad comes here. They are constructing the line not far from us and a station is supposed to be built by the church. They will be looking for labourers.

Рубаєм дерева на сяжень грубі,
Одно два дні довбем, сусіди любі.

Barracks of the first Ukrainian immigrants in Prudentópolis (at that time São João de Capanema), April 1896.

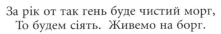

За рік от так гень буде чистий морг,
То будем сіять. Живемо на борг.

Chapter 5 | Memories from the First Waves of Emigration

André Hotzailuk

André Hotzailuk (Andriy Hotsailiuk) was one of many Ukrainians emigrating to Brazil from Galicia's Skalat county, a region where the emigration movement was particularly strong during the first wave. A long-time activist within the Ukrainian community in Prudentópolis, he is most remembered for his work in preserving the culture and traditions of his people in Brazil. Hotzailuk directed the local Ukrainian theatre group during the 1920s and acted in several of its productions. He was one of the first pioneers to write his memoirs. His account, *Spomyny z pershykh khvyl emigratsii*, was published in *Prácia* in 1924.

Who among us does not remember the hardships of the past? Who among us does not remember the fate of the Galician peasant at the end of the last century? And who among us did not experience the injustices of the former Austrian regime in East Galicia, our Polish masters ruling relentlessly and squeezing from us our very last drops of blood and sweat?

It was not strange, then, that the people were interested in leaving for the New World when the first news about Brazil began to circulate through Podillia in 1895. Those who wanted to continue to suffer could stay behind but we knew that we had to look elsewhere for a better life for ourselves and our children. It was August and the decision was made. We would go to Brazil. Many villagers, the cottagers (1) and those of us with some ploughland, decided to leave. The people were saying that there was a lot of land in Brazil and that it was being given away for free. Everyone began to search out the emigration and steamship agents. Some went to the Emigration Office in Lviv. Others went to the St. Raphael Society. Still others wrote to [the city of] Udine to a man named Nodari, sending money and ordering ship tickets. Everyone had caught the emigration fever.

At that time, the [emigration] agency in Lviv was run by Mr. Aleksey Shcherban (2). He sent a transport of emigrants to Brazil in January 1896, accompanying them as they travelled by train to Udine and then to Genoa, Italy, where he was arrested by the police. I was one of the emigrants in this group. Two transports left Galicia in 1895 previous to my departure. I remember everything as if it happened today.

It was January 3, 1896 at about three o'clock in the afternoon when we climbed aboard the train in Pidvolochysk. People from Kachanivka, Supranivka, Mysliv, Orikhovets and other villages in Skalat county were also a part of this transport. Still others, from Luka Velyka and neighbouring villages, boarded in Ternopil.

We arrived at Lviv's Karl Ludwig Station at around ten o'clock that night. The police met us and were there to assist, piling our bags and trunks onto a wagon and taking us to a hotel, the *Zolota Ryba* (3). Soon after we were visited by our agent, Mr. Shcherban, who told us that we would be leaving the city the following morning at 3:00 a.m. It was here at the hotel that we met several other families, also destined for Brazil, who had arrived two days earlier and had been waiting for us.

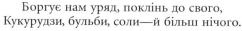

Боргує нам уряд, поклінь до свого,
Кукурудзи, бульби, соли—й більш нічого.

The police arrived at the hotel at the appointed time and took us to the train station. Everyone had to show their documents and money for the trip. We were required to have with us at least 300 *gulden* (4) but there were some of us who did not have even 100. What could we do? But the people looked out for one another and tried to help as they could. After completing the inspection, the same money which had just been shown to the police was carefully passed to the person behind. In this way everyone was able to "produce" the required amount for the trip. Following this we were given our bags and boarded the train, including Mr. Shcherban who was travelling with us. The conductor gave the signal and the train slowly started to move ahead.

How sad this moment was! Everyone had tears in his eyes... Goodbye, native land! Who knows if we will ever see you again! Hey, hey! It was here where we were born and grew up, here where our parents and grandparents lived and worked before us, here where our ancestors toiled under serfdom. This is a land which is so dear to us and yet one which we must leave! Will we ever see you again? Then came the thoughts about what would be waiting for us in Brazil. Would we find a better life there? What will be our fate? Are we going there only to perish? The doubts stuck in everyone's heart and we sat in silent sadness and wiped away the tears.

We travelled from Lviv to Stryi, Budapest and then on to Fiume where we arrived on Christmas Eve (5). We spent some three hours there, getting off the train and walking to a nearby *piazza* where we sat and rested. Some of the people took the opportunity to get some food and eat and Mr. Shcherban even bought candies for the children, this being Christmas Eve. During the stop, the train cars were cleaned because they were dirty and dusty from the trip.

At four o'clock we again boarded the train and continued on to Udine, arriving there that same night. We now travelled on an Italian train which was much cleaner and more comfortable than our Galician one. Our excitement was short-lived, however, because at the following station we were moved to a regular freight car. This was a trip I will never forget. You would wish it upon no one. In spite of the terrible conditions, we arrived safe and sound in the city of Genoa.

Disembarking in Genoa, Mr. Shcherban told us to wait for him at the station while he went to make arrangements for our spending the night in the city and for a hot meal. He warned us several times not to talk to strangers but only to wait. And so there we were, strangers ourselves in a foreign land, downcast and sad. Shortly after, an Italian man came over, showed us some kind of card and then led us like sheep to the pier nearby. When Shcherban appeared some time after, he was so angry that he was almost crying and he scolded us for not waiting as he instructed. Because of our insolence, as he called it, we ended up spending the night at the pier. It was terrible, sleeping on the hard, cold ground and nearly freezing from the wind which was blowing in off the sea. We suffered through the night and in the morning were billeted amongst several private homes where we stayed for a few days. It was here in Genoa that we heard that our agent, Mr. Shcherban, had been arrested.

The next day, we were all called to a neighbourhood chapel where a priest spoke to us in Polish telling us that these were official proceedings regarding the misconduct of Mr. Aleksey Shcherban. We were told that anyone who paid money to Shcherban would be reimbursed and it is true that whoever produced a receipt was given back his money. Some did not want a reimbursement, saying that it had been good travelling with him and he was worth the expense. We were then called to the Brazilian Consulate where we were again required to show our travel documents and were finally given our steamship tickets to Brazil.

On January 11, 1896, we were taken to the pier and led aboard the ship, weighing anchor and pulling away from the shore at about three o'clock in the afternoon. We arrived in Naples the next day at ten o'clock where we stayed for two days, taking on coal, meat, ice and other supplies necessary for the long journey. I remember many Italians also boarded in Naples. We departed on the eve of Yordan (6). During the night there was a terrible storm and the ship was tossed up and down. Everyone suffered terribly from seasickness.

The storm lasted for about a day-and-a-half before finally giving way to calmer waters. Measles ran rampant on board and many children succumbed. Our crossing lasted 22 days and every one of them was marked with a death. By the time we were there, 21 children and one older woman had died.

The day before we arrived in Brazil was marked with much commotion on board. In Genoa, we were joined by a Pole from Sao Mateus, a pharmacist named Luciano Tokarski who was travelling from Italy to Brazil to visit his family. Upon seeing us

Не розлучили нас і на п'ять хвиль...
До міста маємо п'ятнадцять миль.

Ukrainians in our sheepskin coats, he told us not to bring them into the country. The coats surely carried cholera, he said, and would cause us all kinds of problems and detentions at the point of entry. And so, following his advice, more than 100 coats were tossed into the sea! Not everyone listened to that Pole's damned advice and there were no problems in bringing the sheepskin coats into Brazil. In fact, they came to serve the people very well during the cold winter evenings.

We arrived in Rio de Janeiro on the evening of February 3, 1896. After disembarking we were directed onto a Brazilian train and then travelled a day-and-a-half before arriving at the immigration barracks. At one point the train stopped midway through a long tunnel. There was so much smoke inside that we could hardly breathe. Some of the men said sarcastically that it was done on purpose in order to disinfect the cholera in our remaining sheepskin coats. Arriving at our destination we were served a lunch of black beans and rice, potatoes, beef soup and meat, our first meal on Brazilian soil. After lunch we were able to rest after the long trip.

Drying erva mate.

We stayed in these barracks for three full months. The conditions were terrible. How many of our people perished! And not from the cholera which we drowned in the sea with our coats but from yellow fever. There were eight to ten deaths daily. Such crying! Such wailing from the grief-stricken mothers! I myself lost two sons, Mykhailo and Petro, and in my grief I regretted angrily my decision to emigrate. I remember thinking that I had come here to secure a better life, to get some land and here I was burying my children in that same land, so young and so innocent. Many people complained bitterly and said that it would have been better had they never seen this Brazil.

Lenten season arrived. Again homesickness and longing for our native land enveloped us all. We thought about our brothers and sisters attending church in the villages. But here? Nothing of the like. On Good Friday, again with neither a church nor priest, the people could bear no more and something would have to be done. There was an empty room in one of the buildings. We decorated it with palms and other greenery, hung a picture of Christ on the wall, lit candles and were happy for the first time in a long time. How the tears flowed! They poured down the faces of the people. But despair overcame us again as we remembered and longed for our families and native villages.

Easter was marked with bitter tears instead of glad rejoice. Even the poorest of families in Galicia would be attending church and bringing some food for the blessing—at least an egg—but not us. And so, as on Good Friday, we arranged a service for ourselves. We cut some cane to make flagpoles, attached kerchiefs for banners and made a processional cross from bamboo. The procession was ready. We had a couple of cantors in our group and they began to sing *Khrystos Voskres* (7) as they led the procession through the clearings. Two of the men took plates, covered them with kerchiefs and passed them around for a collection. Those who had some money threw it in. The Brazilians were very interested in this and offered their donations. What happened to the money we raised? Just let me say that the cantors drank very well that night. This was our first Easter in Brazil.

A few days later, the emigration director assembled us in his office and had his secretary read off a list of families who would be leaving for Paraná the following day. Everyone was told to be ready for the departure. Those of us remaining

 В лісах під горами... Та ми не ропчем,
Доріг нема, стежки, дасть Бог, протопчем.

comprised a group of about 300 people and by the week's end we had all left for the South. The route took us again to Rio de Janeiro where we boarded a small steamship called the *Vitória* and arrived in [the port city of] Paranaguá within two days. We bypassed the immigration barracks for the train station and after a short trip arrived in Curitiba, the capital of Paraná, by nightfall.

Our stay in Curitiba was short. We were given three meals a day and had some time to look around the city. This was not the Curitiba of today. The trolley, drawn by horses, was already in operation but only along the main streets. The side streets were not any better than we found in Prudentópolis. We stayed in Curitiba for two more days and then travelled by train further inland to Ponta Grossa. Ponta Grossa was a small city. The train line had just been finished and continued no further. We spent a few days here, not in barracks but in rough shelters which had formerly been used as stables. We were responsible for preparing our own meals and it was here that I ate dried meat, *farofa* (8) and black beans for the first time. Our wives did not know how to properly prepare this food but they did their best. They cooked the dried meat into a soup which was so salty that even the dog would not eat it. They boiled the *farofa* into a kind of *kulesha* (9) but it was sour and we could barely bring a taste of it to our mouths.

Some wagons arrived for us after several days in Ponta Grossa and took us by individual family to São João de Capanema, today's Prudentópolis. Prudentópolis is now a proper city but there was only a mud road and a telegraph line when we arrived 28 years ago. An old Brazilian chapel stood where the German church is today. There were a few little houses and all around was the great pinheiro forest. We were taken to our accommodations in the immigration barracks but since there was not enough room for all the people, many built their own shelters from cane and palms with blocks of sod for the roofs. When the rains began, the water immediately leaked through and soaked everything inside. Our suffering continued and again we questioned our fate here.

The *chácaras* (10) had still not been measured out because the surveyors had just arrived. After a couple days of rest the men began work on road construction in order to earn some money for food. We were not used to this kind of work, especially clearing the huge forest which was a monumental task. Road work paid three *mil reis* a day with the first paycheque given after two full weeks of work. Sometimes you would get 45 *mil reis*. Other times only 30.

Everything had to be purchased from the storekeepers who fleeced the poor immigrant at every turn. A 44-kilogram bag of flour cost 45 *mil reis*, a 10 litre bag of beans was 10 *mil reis*, a kilo of sugar cost 1,500, a litre of salt 1, 10 litres of corn flour 5, manioc flour 3, a kilo of coffee 3, a kilo of salt pork also 3 and so on. You should remember that the *mil reis* was worth something at that time. Those immigrants with large families were unable to support themselves with the money earned from construction. Many Ukrainians died from starvation. Add to this typhus and yellow fever and there were at least 15 deaths occurring daily. There were not even enough boards for the coffins. I myself remember one family of eight, seven of whom died from hunger leaving only the father surviving.

A Ukrainian Catholic church near Prudentópolis.

Та ви цікаві, як нам до води,
Доїхалось, а потім сюди.

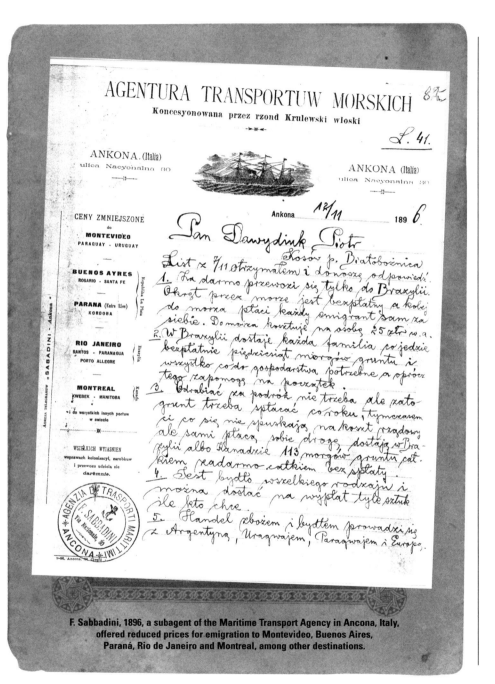

F. Sabbadini, 1896, a subagent of the Maritime Transport Agency in Ancona, Italy, offered reduced prices for emigration to Montevideo, Buenos Aires, Paraná, Rio de Janeiro and Montreal, among other destinations.

In such misery, many parents sold their children into work service for more affluent families while others traded them for a bag of flour. Young girls quickly lost their innocence. Children were born and died without baptism because of the lack of priests. A member of the secular clergy and his wife arrived in June of that year but did not stay very long. It was not clear if he left on his own or if the government ordered his departure because married priests were not allowed in Brazil at that time. It was not until the arrival of Father Nykon Rozdolsky from Galicia that the people realized that God had not completely forgotten them. Rozdolsky stayed with us for some time and worked hard at establishing a church. Not having our own chapel, we used the old Brazilian one which was now barely standing. But our happiness was short-lived as the bishop soon reassigned Rozdolsky to the colony of Rio Claro.

We remained without a priest for almost two years. Those who wanted to get married had to travel on foot to the city of Cupim some seven miles away. During this time some of the people began settling on their *chácaras* while others remained in their huts in Prudentópolis. We had now been here for nine months and the Brazilian government was no longer providing support. Rumours were spreading that the immigrants would be sent back to Galicia. Some of the settlers, believing the stories, waited for the steamships to arrive and in so doing wasted precious time. Everyone suffered from terrible poverty. There was no food, no money, no work. The people ate *pinhões* (11) and the soft centres of palm trees, [the so-called palm cabbage]. They also collected mushrooms, many dying from the poisonous ones which were just as common here as in the old country.

These events took place between May 1896 and January 1897. Some of the immigrants also brought vegetable seeds with them but this was not planting season and they were not familiar with the Brazilian way of cultivating the soil. Some had planted rye by 1897, having purchased the seed grain from the storekeeper because the Brazilian government no longer provided assistance. We suffered terribly and little by little despair overcame everyone. The people arrived believing they would find a better life here but were met with only difficulties, sickness, hunger and such terrible poverty… Death was everywhere and families dissolved as husbands buried their wives, wives buried their husbands and everyone had buried at least one child. There was no joy, no hope and no clergy to offer the spiritual comfort which would encourage and inspire the people to keep

 До Відня їхали спокійно, вкупі,
У Відні нас три дні держали цюпі.

them going. In their misery some of the men damned Brazil. And who knows what would have happened to us had God in His mercy not sent us our angel from Heaven in the person of Father Sylvester Kizyma?

Kizyma arrived in Prudentópolis (then São João de Capanema) on January 20, the very day of St. John the Baptist, and, after a short rest from the long journey, began his missionary work. People came from all around to hear the word of God. Spirits were raised, there was new hope in the arrival of this young priest and everyone began to look towards a brighter future. The people were happier and worked hard. Father Sylvester offered much help and encouragement but, as with each of God's shepherds, he faced obstacles and opponents at every turn.

Having been without the care of the church for so long, many people lost their faith and morale had fallen terribly. Children were working as servants and young girls had taken an immoral path. Everything changed with Father Sylvester's arrival. Parents began taking their children out of service to others and the girls recognized the error of their ways. Others searched out and reclaimed the children they had sold off.

There was great opposition to Father Sylvester as the people returned to the teachings of God and things began to improve. He was threatened by some of the immoral and faithless souls among us who destroyed his living quarters next to the Brazilian chapel and said that they would kill him unless he stopped his teachings. He was not intimidated and only continued his work.

In time, Father Sylvester began visiting other Ukrainian colonies, travelling by foot and then by horse. Since there were still no chapels, services were conducted in the settlers' houses. It is no exaggeration that Prudentópolis and the surrounding colonies would not be what they are today if it were not for the work of Father Sylvester and his successors.

Father Sylvester Kizyma, OSBM, the first Ukrainian Catholic missionary to serve in Brazil. He arrived in Curitiba on June 21, 1897.

Arriving to help Father Sylvester were Father Martyniuk and Brother Horoshchuk who built a chapel, founded the Brotherhood of the Sacred Heart of Jesus and established a school. The first teacher was Mr. Kazymyr Brodziak and then Mr. Ivan Lekh. Many children attended school as did the older married people who recognized the need and importance of education. The amateur theatre group was founded by Mr. Lekh and became so loved and so popular that you could hardly keep the people away. The first presentation was *Nich Vyfleyemska* (12).

The presentations continued, the people embraced enlightenment and education and their souls were raised up. But as always, there were some problems. A play during *Carnaval* (13) one year was disrupted by some of the locals who did not understand what we were doing and began to taunt the people. They threw lassos around their necks and tried to lead them off like cattle. In the evening, many of these daredevils wanted to attend the production but they were kept away. What is more, our boys gave them a good thrashing for their trouble. The priests suffered through a lot in those early years and yet they were our greatest helpers, organizers of schools, churches and community life. The Ukrainian people have not forgotten this and remain thankful for all that they have done.

Пустили нас, лиш пан якийсь від нас,
Сім срібла взяв, що підписав пас.

Chapter 6: In Search of a Better Life

Felipe Kobrên

Felipe Kobrên (Pylyp Kobryn) was 14 years old when he and his family emigrated to Brazil in 1896 and settled near Iracema in Paraná's neighbouring state of Santa Catarina. He was living in Três Barras-Tigre at the time he wrote his memoirs. Throughout his life was one of the area's most dedicated community activists. He was the first schoolteacher in the colony of Antônio Olinto, he served as choir director and conducted services at the church in Iracema in the absence of the priest. Kobrên's memoirs, dated August 25, 1935, were published in *Prácia* the following year on the occasion of the fortieth anniversary of the Ukrainian emigration to Brazil, 1895-1935.

It was in the first days of July 1896 that we said goodbye to our native village of Ostalovychi, Peremyshliany county. The misery, poverty and difficulties had made the decision for us, forcing us from our home in search of a better life in the at that time much-praised Brazil. We were among seven families, 24 people in all, emigrating from our village. Four of the families left a few weeks earlier with the rest of us following in July. Nearly 40 years have passed since we arrived in Brazil and saw for the first time the impassable forests whose trails were trod only by the wild Brazilian Indians, the *bugres* (1).

It was in the months of June and July of 1896 that the people began leaving en masse for Brazil. No one even asked what would be waiting for him there but everyone knew that it could surely be no worse than in the old country. Everyone was so poor. It was even more difficult for those without a job. With little exception, the manor workers and the cottagers (2), as they were called, almost died from hunger. In addition to food they also had to buy provisions for winter such as firewood, warm clothing and good boots. They had to pay house, land, road and military taxes and other expenses which they could not afford. Those who did not have the money would lose the shirts off their backs and then freeze in winter. It was this poverty which ultimately drove our people across the ocean where they believed life would be better.

In Galicia the lords and the Jews sat on thousands of acres of land, eating and drinking in great banquets while our poor peasant did not even have a place to rest his head. Some of the people who made the decision to emigrate had a little mud-plastered house, two or three *morgs* of land, but with eight, ten or 12 people inside who needed to be fed and clothed, they had no choice but to leave. Even the more well-to-do peasants with ten to 12 *morgs* of land were leaving, saying, "I have some land but what will my children have after I'm gone?" It was true. And so they went to Brazil, to this country beyond the mountains and across the sea in search of a better life so that it would be better for their children…

We travelled by train from Lviv through Kraków and Vienna to the Italian city of Udine and from there to the port city of Genoa where we boarded a steamship by the same name. There were many Italians travelling with us. They looked at us and we looked at them but we were strangers to one another. The captain of the ship and all of his crew were Italians. The captain himself was an older man, strong as a bear, often scowling, sullen, serious and a man of not many words. I saw him once when he came to reprimand two of our boys for scrapping. He said a couple of strong words and then took the two wrestlers to cool off.

 З Понтеби завернули нас до Грацу.
Там три неділі мали з нами працю.

The beginnings of Ukrainian settlement in the municipality of Prudentópolis.

Писали до Стрия, Мостів і Кут,
А нам казали—«Зачекайте тут!»

Leaving Genoa, we continued on our voyage, sailing on open seas directly to Rio de Janeiro. The crossing lasted a full three weeks, or 21 days if you prefer. What did the people do with themselves on board? The days were spent mostly on deck. We Ruthenians tended to stay amongst ourselves as did our fellow travellers, the *taliany* (3). There was no other way. We did not understand each other and to us, their language was just incoherent mumbling.

We were given three meals a day. The food was good but we did not spend a lot of time eating. Some people did not eat at all because they were ill. This was the so-called seasickness which affected everyone who was travelling by ship for the first time. They would say to me "We are going to die here and never even see Vobrazylia! (4) Why did we make this trip?" More time was spent on the distribution of the meals than on eating the food itself. The kitchen had one muddle-headed fellow who would run with the trays to serve the people as fast as he could. More than one meal ended up on the floor. I remember another server who slipped and dropped everything he was carrying. Whoever was lucky enough to get his meal would sit down without ceremony and begin eating. There were no tables or benches and so everyone sat on the floor to eat.

The rest of the time was spent in various ways. Some relaxed and listened to stories. We had some excellent storytellers among us who in three weeks of travelling did not manage to exhaust their repertoires. Some read or wrote letters. Others amused themselves by playing cards, dominoes or the violin. Some of the people stood on deck and watched the ocean, the water, the ship and the fish. There were some among us who just prayed. One day one of the men announced loudly, "Hey, people, do you know what day it is today?" It became silent and then someone answered, "How would we know what day it is today when we have lost track of the time here at sea?" "Today," he said, "is a holy day. The month of August. The sixth day. Today is *Spasa*." (5)

Everyone knelt down and prayed "Our Father, who art in Heaven…" They began to read the psalm "Praise the Name of God" (*Velychanie*) and sing other religious songs. The people stood and prayed as if they were in church. The women wept openly and the men too were seen wiping their tears. And it was not without reason. They remembered their village churches, their family and friends with whom they lived, worked and prayed. They remembered their priest who blessed them as they set out on this unknown journey. The memories flooded in and reduced them to tears… Our fellow travellers, the *taliany*, who were now standing closer to us, removed their hats, knelt down and prayed with us even though they did not understand anything of our songs or prayers. They knew that we believed in God and whether theirs or ours, it was the same God. It was strange to us that they did not have a similar celebration.

And so passed the days one after another. Everyone became very anxious after about a week-and-a-half at sea. Most spent the days up on deck and then made their way down the stairs at night where they slept on bunk beds which were stacked several high. Families were separated for sleeping. The men and boys slept together in one common room below deck and the women, girls and infants in another…

Some days were more interesting than others. Among the *taliany*, who travelled with us, there were often disputes, arguments and fights such that the ship's crew members had rather a lot of work with their fellow countrymen. We never knew what the problems were. We did not understand their language but we did learn a great many of their words. Our people, except for the one incident with the boys' wrestling, behaved themselves well and there were no such problems. You might say that we Ruthenians by nature are not as hot-blooded, perhaps because the sun shines more intensely in Italy than it does in Galicia.

While the Italians were arguing and fighting, our people were singing. And so it began. One or two people at first. Then before you knew it 100 or 200 people had joined their voices together. This was not a proper choir in three- or four-part harmony but there were as many wonderful voices as there were participants. The melodies were beautiful! The baritones and basses of the men and the sopranos of the women, as delicate as the meowing of kittens, produced a wonderful sound.

There were no conductors, no sheet music and no previous rehearsals but the mix of voices was so beautiful that you just wanted to listen. What did they sing? Anything and everything they knew. In addition to church and religious songs, they also performed folk and popular ones. They did very well, our poor and forlorn travellers, who, instead of crying, squabbling or wallowing in their homesickness, sang from the very bottom of their souls…

Палазя там умерла від уроків,
А лікар німець мовив—«З браку солів.»

There were other adventures at sea with some women giving birth on board the ship. The parents were so happy even though these were difficult times. They selected godparents in anticipation of the christening but there was no priest among us and it was still a far way off to Brazil. I know one woman until today who gave birth on the ship. These events were joyful for some but sad and full of tears for others. Some of the newborns died, an event which filled everyone, not only the parents and family, with such sadness. Funerals were held but the ceremonies were performed without a priest and without the rituals of the old country. Instead of coffins and a proper burial, the bodies were thrown into the sea. The people just stood and watched, staring at the water as the sadness lingered long after...

The voyage quickly tired us. We would have welcomed the sight of land by the first week of sailing and here it was the end of the second week and the Brazilian shores were still far in the distance. In the evenings the people would ask, "Do you know how far it is to Vobrazylia?" But there was really no one to ask, other than ourselves. No one else understood our language. There was an interpreter on board who could help us with such questions but where would we find him among so many people? By the third week—I do not recall the exact day—we saw some large birds flying overhead which perched themselves on the ship's masts. Land was still nowhere in sight but we knew that it must not be far off. These birds provided some good entertainment. They would fly high above the sea and then dive straight into the water, beating their wings furiously on the surface before flying back out. They were fishing for food which they would then swallow in one gulp. Their skills were amazing.

A congregation in front of the church in Antônio Olinto, Paraná.

The following day we saw land in the distance. The ship began to reduce its speed and we were now sailing slowly. Some more land came into view. These were small coastal islands and we sailed so close to one of them that you could see the trees on shore. The ship was now moving very slowly and passing by the islands. It was afternoon. I do not remember if it was the same day or the next but we had finally arrived at the port of Rio de Janeiro. There was hardly any noise as we pulled into the harbour but then the ship began to groan so loudly before it stopped that you could barely hear yourself think.

We saw many things for the first time in our lives here in Rio, especially people of different colour. Some were like smoked sausage, some were the colour of bread

Івась умер напевно від нічниць,
А лікар мовив—«Не плетіть дурниць!»

baked in the clay oven, others were like scorched buckwheat groats and still others as black as our old-country iron cooking pots. Oh, how we looked at them! But they looked at us the same way! When we arrived in Rio de Janeiro we were wearing our woollen overcoats, shirts of homespun linen, jackets, wide trousers, wide leather belts, big boots, big hats, some had sheepskin coats... The women were dressed in printed skirts, sashes, coral beads and their unusual headdresses... The girls with their hair in long braids, wearing brightly coloured ribbons and corsets... So tell me, was there not something for them to stare at?! Who here had ever seen such things?!

As soon as the ship stopped, a cloud of native Brazilians came up with oranges, bananas and other fruits, calling out, *"Senhores, quem quer comprar laranjas, bananas?"* (6) We replied to them, "Hey! What are you saying? What's that pretty one? What does it cost?" We tried our best to understand and did buy some of the fruit.

Having arrived, we were told that our baggage had been collected and was ready to be claimed. That same evening some men from the city, carrying books and papers, came to see us. They travelled on a little steamship, coming on board our ship and making their way to the authorities. Our people, in meeting these men, removed their hats, bowed and greeted them with "Glory to God and Jesus Christ!" to which they replied in their own language *"Boa tarde"* (7). This was our last night on the ship and after the evening meal we collected our baggage so that we would be ready for disembarking the next day. No one could sleep. We stood on deck and looked at the city. It was still off in the distance. It was a dark night and we could see nothing but the glimmering of the street lamps and other city lights. We were glad that our long voyage had ended and that tomorrow we would finally be on land.

The night passed quickly. It was very late when we went to sleep and we were awake before dawn. We were told to take our baggage to the exit. With this arose a great confusion. Parents watched carefully that their children did not get lost, something which would have been very easy in the chaos of the moment, and so families were instructed to stay together.

We began leaving the ship. Families disembarked one by one and no other people could leave until they had done so entirely. The Italians were first to leave followed by us *austriacos* or Galicians or Ruthenians or Russians or Poles as we were called. A set of stairs was attached to the ship so that we could exit onto large boats. These boats, connected to one another in a long line and pulled by a small steamship, would transport us from ship to shore. I do not remember how many there were in all. To help us in getting on and to keep anyone from falling into the water, there were two men providing assistance. One stood at the base of the stairs and the other at the entrance to the boat. Women were usually helped on board first, followed by the children and then the men. This was the first time in my life that I had seen such strong men, at times lifting even the heaviest passenger and effortlessly placing him into the boat.

With everyone safely on board, a whistle blew and we began to move quietly along the water towards the shore. A lively conversation immediately began. This was the New World. We had arrived in a new city. There were so many ships around us. Smaller and larger vessels. And other people, other voices and other languages. It was all so interesting for us. It was a short trip and I do not know if even an hour had passed before we finally arrived at the shore…

The Italians seemed to know how everything worked but we still did not. After all, it had been their port of departure, their ship and their crew. There was already an established Italian community in Brazil, with their own people, their own organizations and their own immigration society when they arrived here. We remembered some of the people from our St. Raphael Society in Lviv who, with the exception of a few, did not even know where this Vobrazylia was, whether in Asia or Africa or somewhere else. At that time we Ruthenians knew only that this was a largely unsettled land with a small population. That was all we knew about Brazil.

Our disembarking in Rio de Janeiro did not take very long, maybe only a few minutes. We proceeded to the station where the train had been waiting for us and we boarded immediately. The train cars were quickly filled and packed tightly with people. With everyone in place, the crew began giving out bread and meat, saying *"Pão e carne"* as they passed it out. We did not know what they were saying but we took it anyway because we were so hungry. Previous to our disembarking from the ship, we had not eaten nor drunk anything.

Bells rang. A whistle blew. The train began to make noise and pulled away from the station. We were travelling once again but this time on land. Brazilian land. The sun had already set. The Italians travelled together in their cars and we in ours. There

Так як ще Гриць, Оксанка, Рузя вмерли,
Пустили нас—«Ідіть, куди наперли!»

were so many people that there was barely a passageway to walk through. We left Rio de Janeiro not even having seen this city, Brazil's largest. No one was too concerned, though. Everyone was thinking—is it still far to our land? how much land will they give us? will there be forest and firewood which was in such short supply in the old country? would our misery finally be over? what is the name of this city? is it big? and so many more questions.

...All of the windows were open and yet there was still such sweltering heat inside the train cars. At first the people looked out the windows at the orange groves, the gardens, the countryside, the forest. Everything was so different from home. We arrived at the first station. The second. And then so many more. The train stopped for two to three minutes at each one and then continued on... Each station had a large sign which read *Estrada de Ferro Central do Brasil*. The words *do Brasil* were for many so confusing. We were already here in Brazil and yet we were going to Brazil? (8)

The sun was high. The children were hungry and were given a few bites of bread and meat. The drinking water was cold and, while they could have had more, it satisfied them. They were bored, irritable and started to cry. They wanted to nurse but their mothers, having eaten only dry bread these last few days, had nothing for them to suckle. Although we ate well on the steamship, the food was poor on the train. The first hours of the trip were new and interesting for us and we were captivated by the sights of the Brazilian environment. After awhile, however, the novelty wore off. The midday heat was unbearable. The cars were crowded, dusty and smelled of smoke. Hunger, heat and exhaustion kept us from sleeping. It was worst of all for the young ones. The poor mothers wept because they were unable to comfort their children. It was just as difficult for the fathers.

The train continued on, stopping for only a few minutes and blowing its whistle at each station. No one knew how much longer it would be. Finally around two o'clock in the afternoon the train let out a long whistle as we pulled up in front of some big buildings and came to a stop. We were instructed to get off the train, take our baggage with us and proceed inside. Families waited together, setting down their bags and sitting or lying on the floor to rest. There were no benches or beds. Some of the women spread out a *plakhta* (9) or got some pillows to make it more comfortable.

The building was soon full of people. There were perhaps hundreds in this one great room and yet it offered a refreshing coolness. With the people assembled inside, we were called for lunch. The *taliany* went first and we waited until they finished because there was not enough room at the tables for everyone. We ate about an hour later. We were so hungry. This was our first meal on Brazilian soil. The Brazilian government continued to cover our expenses as they had done since our departure from Europe. The voyage cost us nothing. The expenses for our food and lodgings for the three weeks we stayed here were also covered by the government... It was during our stay here in [the city of] Pinheiro that we walked for the first time on Brazilian soil, saw the forests, countryside and rivers. It was the first time that we ate black beans, rice and the local meat. It was also the first time that we rested after a long and tiring voyage...

Brazilian Indians, near Prudentópolis.

До моря ми дібрались без біди,
Лиш що до нас присілись два жиди.

...It was good for our immigrants in Pinheiro (10). They ate, drank and relaxed, most of them never in their lives having enjoyed such pleasures. There were few worries because everyone knew that he would be getting some land. The people did not even have to prepare their own food. The cooks—and there were many of them, mostly native Brazilians—had a lot of work in the kitchen. Some of our women offered their help and it was gladly accepted. A bell was rung at meal times and everyone would proceed into the dining room and sit at long marble tables. The cooks served us, bringing everything right to the tables. We were treated like guests at a banquet. Breakfast was usually coffee and some buns. Lunch and dinner were the standard Brazilian offerings. It was a custom here to add *farofa*, corn or manioc flour, to the beans but our people did not know how to do this. The cooks found it odd that we were not eating the flour and so they showed us how to mix it into the beans.

Our lodgings in Pinheiro were encircled by a steel fence. It was impossible to go over or through it. A steel gate opened onto the yard and a gatekeeper or guard usually sat there day and night. It was closed and locked from nine o'clock in the evening until the next morning, allowing no one entry or exit. We were free to go where we pleased during the day—to the station, to the *venda* (11) or elsewhere for a walk. There was a large river nearby, fed by a smaller one, with the immigration buildings located at their junction. One of the buildings was a hospital. I was 14 years old at the time and did not take too much of an interest in the buildings. The other boys and I usually went walking in the forest, swimming in the river or spent time at the train station.

The *taliany* did not remain too long with us here, leaving for São Paulo after several days. We too were approached by some individuals who wanted to send us to São Paulo but we had been informed by the St. Raphael Society to tell everyone that we were intent on going to Paraná.

Our time in Pinheiro was also marked with some tragedies. One day some of the men went swimming in the river. One of them, a strapping young man, slipped off his clothes and dived into the water as we stood on the shore and watched. We looked to see where he would come up but we did not see him. Soon after you could see bubbles breaking at the surface but then nothing more. A group of people jumped in and began searching for him but he

Carroças (Brazilian-style farm wagons) making their way through the forest

І видурили від Баланди і Хмиза,
По десять ринських за якісь авіза.

could not be found. It was so sad to see his grief-stricken parents who had delighted in their only son as their greatest blessing in life. But now he was gone. His poor mother was screaming, "My son! My son! Where are you?!" She fell down, rolling around on the ground in her grief... His body was found and buried a few days later...

...To pass their time here, the people would take walks or go to the station or the *venda* to listen to the local language and observe the people. Some tried hunting in the forest. Others swam. Those who stayed behind would read, tell stories or partake in lively discussions. Some of the men played their instruments, the violin or the bass, while others danced the traditional *kolomyika*, *trambulianka* or *kozak*. A large group would invariably be there to watch, not only our people but the Brazilians too. Even the immigration officials watched with interest. The local Brazilians had never seen such dancing, saying, *"Eles sabem dançar bonito!"* (12)

The people, anxious and eager to keep moving, began asking the immigration officials why they were being held here for so long. "Please let us continue," they would say, "so that no more time will be wasted!" They waited two more days after the inquiry. A train arrived. Something was happening. A man came and spoke to us in Polish, saying that we would be continuing on. Such confusion ensued as everyone began collecting his possessions, packing pillows, trunks and clothing, and bringing them to the train. Women carried children in both arms with the others behind them in tow. The train started to move and we were once again on our way. Our Polish speaking friend was travelling with us. We asked him if we were going to São Paulo and he replied, "Ladies and gentlemen, we are going to the province *[sic]* of Paraná!"

The train, not counting the two-to-three-minute stops at each station, travelled quickly. We had arrived back at the sea and were transported immediately to a small steamship. We boarded, settled in and fell right to sleep. This time it was only we Ruthenians on board—there were no Italians—and we travelled through the night and the whole next day before arriving. At midday we were served the usual meal of black beans and rice, but there were little white worms swimming in the pot. One man remarked that they looked like our old-country salt pork cracklings. Someone took a plateful to show the cook who only laughed and said, *"Coma, coma, não faz mal, nós todos comemos assim mesmo."* (13)

...We arrived later that same day and spent the night in some kind of a large shed. As we found out at breakfast the following morning, this was the city of Paranaguá. We spent another day and night here and then left by train the next day. The stations passed by quickly. We travelled through forest, rock and scenery the likes of which we had never seen back home. Who in Peremyshliany, Bibrka or Ternopil counties had ever seen this before?! The jungles gave way to a larger city. The sign at the station read Curitiba. "What was this *Tsuritiba*?" as we pronounced it (14).

A Ukrainian wedding in Brazil. Seated, the bride and bridegroom, Maria Petryk and João Homeniuk.

Та на одній переїздці якось,
Згубився і пропав Юрків Антось.

Getting off the train, we were directed to our accommodations in the city. It was a wooden building with the names and surnames of those people who had been here before us written on the wall boards. They had since left the city and gone on to their colonies. We recognized some names from our village of Ostalovychi but we could not find out where they went. We were so happy that some of our people were already here. We had the opportunity to meet with some Polish immigrants in *Tsuritiba* who had settled here previously. Every Pole welcomed us as he would his own brother. The whole city was foreign to us but the Poles helped us as they could. We learned, for example, that *chácaras* were only given to those who were married. So our people began to make matches and marry off their children—even those who were underage. The young people did not seem to mind this and their parents were happy that their children—and their children's children—would be able to have land of their own. You did not waste time on ceremony. The older people acted as matchmakers, the young people quickly got to know each other, they got married and *está pronto* (15). The elders regretted that the weddings were performed without the traditions of the plaiting of the bridal wreaths, dowries and presentations of gifts. But they did have music, especially our *kolomyika, kozak* and the Seven Step.

At that time the city of Curitiba was small, not like the city it is today. Old style houses with earthen walls stood where the Praça Tiradentes is now. The electric trolley system was implemented later. Today's Campo de Galícia was then only swamps and marshes. No people lived there. Only frogs and snakes.

After spending several days in Curitiba, we were taken by train to Rio Negro where we stayed for a few more days. We tried to orient ourselves to the city, we looked around and were taken to the banks of the river by the same name. There was a thick forest on the other side and crossings were done by ferry boat since there were still no bridges. Rio Negro was surrounded by forest and the settlement itself was just a little clearing in the middle with a few wooden houses. Horses, pigs and chickens walked everywhere.

We had been provided with food up until now but from here on we were responsible for our own meals. Every family was given a month's supply of black beans, wheat flour, rice, manioc flour, sugar, coffee and salt. The people began cooking for themselves, making *pyrohy*, boiled dough, *lemishka* and so on. The women said that they had nothing with which to roll *holubtsi* or to make *borshch* (16). There were no ovens to bake bread.

Receiving our supplies, some large *carroças* (17) with four, six or eight horses came and transported us further into the forest. The women, children and all the baggage were put on the *carroças* and the men and the older children walked behind. There was not enough room for everyone. The road passed through a sort of underground tunnel. The sun hardly shone through and there were mud puddles everywhere. It was difficult to keep going with the horses and *carroças* and walking was no easier. We had boots on our feet but so much mud stuck to thoem that it seemed like four or five kilos of weight had been added to each foot. We truly believed that there was no end to this road—or this forest—and we were so tired.

Night was falling. Where would we sleep? In the mud puddles? Late at night we came upon a clearing in the forest, a "city" as they called it, made up of a few houses. It had what sounded like a woman's name, Lucena. This is today's city of Itaiópolis in Santa Catarina. At that time there was only one house, that which belonged to the immigration officials. The rest of the buildings were just miserable shelters. We spent that first night outside but then they began to build a shelter for us from bamboo. We stayed there for several days. We would make a large fire for cooking the meals and several women would prepare their food and place it in pots around the edge... We did not sit at proper tables, as in Pinheiro, but ate all together from one large bowl as they used to do in the old country.

We had a lot of trouble with the meals as I recall. It often happened that the fire would go out or the wood was not completely dry and it made more smoke than anything else. The nights were so dark—there were no other lights—and so you often ate in complete darkness. The immigration officials provided every family with the following tools–an axe, a hoe, a *foice* and a shovel. One cross-cut or other large saw was shared among several families.

We had food and tools. Now we just needed some land. We were told that it had still not been measured out and we would have to wait. A couple of weeks passed before the land was surveyed and distributed. Each family was given one *chácara*—or ten *alqueires*. In coming here we found several Polish settlements such as those in São Paulo, São Pedro, São João and Santo Antônio. They had been settled here for several years already and were doing well.

В Геневі ми сім неділь шифу ждали,
За містом в порах як цигани спали.

Soon after we were at work with our axes, foices and saws. We began to fell trees and clear land in today's colony of Iracema and other neighbouring Ukrainian *linhas*. More or less at this same time the settlers began clearing land in the colonies of Prudentópolis, Dorizon, Mallet, Antônio Olinto and others. Today, some 40 years later, it is because of the work and sacrifice of our people that the great expanses of Brazilian forest, once inhabited only by Indians, wild animals, dangerous snakes and spiders, have been replaced by fields of farmland, houses and settlements, domesticated animals, orchards and gardens.

Brazil. This was the promised land for us. We give thanks to God, first of all, for watching over us as we made the voyage. We give thanks to our parents and families for bringing us here and for providing the opportunity for a better life. We give thanks to the Brazilian government for allowing and helping us to settle here.

São Paulo Railway's Paranapiacaba Station, one of the immigrants' last stops before reaching their destinations.

Поганий край! Докучив голод нам,
І гарячок понабирались там.

Chapter 7: In the Paths of Many

Miguel Cheuczuk

Miguel Cheuczuk (Mykhailo Shevchuk) emigrated to Brazil with his family in 1896 and settled in the colony of Antônio Olinto (then called Água Amarela), Paraná. Like Kobrên, Cheuczuk's memoirs were written on the occasion of the fortieth anniversary of Ukrainian settlement in Brazil and published in *Prácia* in 1936.

We lived in the village of Obarynets, county of Ternopil. There were six of us in our family, me, my two brothers, my sister and my middle-aged parents. A rumour was circulating around the village about this place called Brazil and some gentleman—a steamship agent, that is—was making a list of people who wanted to emigrate. The villagers were consulting with each other and did not know what to do. Some of the Jewish men had put such fear into the people that only one family—ours—decided to emigrate.

As I remember, it was summer vacation from school. My father came home one day and told us the unexpected news: we were leaving for Brazil. He explained to us that the conditions at home were forcing us to go to another country in order to make a better life for the family. There was only poverty, unemployment, and with father's total of four *morgs* of farmland, the future held no promise for any of us.

I remember my brother and me jumping for joy! And we talked about nothing else, only this. We asked father when we would be leaving, the route which we would take and when we would arrive. Other people tried to scare us with tales of savages, snakes, jungle animals and insects but we paid no attention. A merchant came from Ternopil one day and bought our house and land.

Our departure was approaching. We would be leaving for Brazil in three days and the evenings were filled with farewells as the village priest, the teacher and friends came to say their goodbyes. Finally it was the last day. More friends and neighbours came to the house to see us off. There were still so many people but it was getting late and we had to go. With two wagons waiting, we piled on our possessions, climbed in and started to move ahead. This was the last time we would see our house, our church or our school.

We reached the station in Ozirna by morning. The train arrived shortly after and we continued on to the city of Ternopil. Five other families from the neighbouring village and another Jewish gentleman were making the trip with us. We travelled from Ternopil to Lviv where we stayed for a whole week. We finally boarded a train for Vienna, crossing the Austrian border and stopping in the Italian city of Udine. I still remember the long tunnels and the beautiful Austrian Alps as if it were just yesterday and yet 40 years have since passed.

We travelled from Udine to the port of Genoa where we met many others [from Galicia] who had arrived before us. It was in October when we left and I remember the sun baking down mercilessly. We boarded the ship at night. Our sleeping quarters were located below deck but it was so hot that you could barely breathe. We lay down but it was impossible to sleep because of the heat and the fleas.

In the morning we heard such noises! A crash, a roar and we were already well out to sea by the time we went on deck and looked around. You could see neither a city

Сім штук дітей, Онищиха й Чаплиха,
І Хрущ старий там вмерли. Збулись лиха.

A Ukrainian family in Prudentópolis.

 Було б нас більше померло, бо якась,
На нас якась італьська пані завязлась.

nor any land, only sky and the great expanse of water. Our ship moved with great momentum as it cut through the enormous waves. The first few days were without incident but then the people began to get seasick. The food lost its taste and keeping anything in your stomach became difficult, if not impossible.

Before long, we passed Spain and were now out in the great ocean. The ship would rock terribly at times. The Italians on board treated us very well and gave us good meals. Sundays and holidays were spent in quiet contemplation as the people remembered their village, their church, their home. But here? There was nothing of the like. Only the sky and the endless sea. We were already so very homesick.

From time to time we would pass by little islands and then see a spot in the distance which would get larger as we approached. This was another island and our ship stopped and threw in the anchor as we came closer. Smaller boats took us ashore where we met many other Ukrainians who had arrived before us. I remember it was here that we saw black people for the first time in our lives. Some of us were afraid of them, while others stared with great interest. Almost immediately a bell rang calling us for dinner. We sat behind marble tables while black cooks served us beans and rice. I remember the beans were full of little white worms and the people, never having seen *faryna* (1) before, thought it was sawdust.

We observed the Brazilian scenery with great interest. Some of the men made themselves reed flutes, *sopilky* (2), from bamboo and played music in order to lighten the mood. On Sundays the people would gather in the shade and sing religious songs. It had been three weeks already since we left Genoa. We stayed in the barracks for almost a month and managed to settle in rather quickly. When we received word that we would be moving on, we were transported by boat to the pier in Rio de Janeiro, boarding a Brazilian ship and sailing along the coast to Paranaguá.

At night we were seized by a terrible storm which threw the small ship around as if it were a little splinter in the water. The storm finally stopped and we arrived safely in Paranaguá, spending the night there and travelling by train to Curitiba early the next day. Our stop in Curitiba was short, just a few hours, before we continued on to Lapa where large freight wagons were already waiting for us. We loaded on our baggage, climbed aboard and were taken to an abandoned brickyard located past the city. We spent the night there. We were so hungry and cold because there were no walls, just a roof, and the inside was full of manure and other filth. We suffered through that first night but made our way to the city as soon as morning broke so that we could buy something to eat, especially for the little ones. Thankfully, the Brazilian government began giving out food to the people.

We spent three weeks in Lapa. I remember hunting birds and animals and running away when we saw a lizard for the first time because we thought it was a monster! Roads were being built through the forest so that it would be possible to travel further inland. We again made our way by wagon. The drivers were from Germany and since some of our people could speak German, they were able to have a proper conversation. We travelled for two days before arriving at a location called Água Amarela where we were divided up among some empty houses until a road could be cleared for us to continue further. We spent several days here. The Brazilians often came to see us but, not knowing Portuguese, we were unable to speak with them.

Narodnyi Dim (Ukrainian National Home) in Prudentópolis.

«І випросила в короля свідоцтво—
«Держать їх, аж їм вмре жіноцтво.»

Nauka—to syla. (Education is power.) A Ukrainian schoolhouse near Prudentópolis from the first years of settlement. In front, the teacher and his students pose for the photographer before beginning the day's lessons.

Хрест божий з нами! Певно се була,
Якась безбожна упириця зла.

A road had been cleared but it was so narrow that a wagon could barely pass through. This was a dark, thick forest full of animals like wild pigs, monkeys and even small tigers. The people were terribly afraid when they heard the pigs' growling noises. Many thought that it was the roar of a lion!

Our journey continued as we were transported by wagons to a place called Metves. It was impossible to go any further because the bridges had not yet been built. The people made some barracks from rough boards. They erected a wooden cross in a small clearing where they gathered on Sundays to pray and conduct services on their own. Our settlement was located about four kilometres away from the colony of Antônio Olinto. As the *shakry* were numbered and distributed, my father claimed one for himself. It was located close to the centre of the settlement and he and my eldest brother immediately went out to clear a piece of land where we put up a temporary house. They cleared another patch, burned the stumps and planted corn and beans even though it was already too late in the season.

Now the poverty began! Such complete and utter poverty! By this time the government had ended the distribution of provisions to the settlers. The people went out and started to cut down trees but they were not used to this kind of work. Our mother took ill and died within a few days. Such sadness! Such hunger! We now had to manage for ourselves but none of us knew how to wash clothes or prepare food! My brother and I were finally forced to leave our father and go far away to work for the *caboclos* (3) where we stayed for about three years.

The people did not remain in the barracks for very long. They began resettling in the surrounding colonies, leaving behind their wooden cross which still stands to this day. They lived close together and, as more Ukrainian and Polish immigrants continued to arrive, there soon were so many people that we began to look like ants in an anthill. The more well-to-do settlers began building better houses and even a few stores.

By this time everyone had received a *shakra*. The government officials began telling the people to make their way to their land and begin working on it because supplies of food were no longer being provided. Some of the people had not done anything in terms of settling themselves and said that the government was still obliged to give them food. Others did not know how or when to begin planting. Many simply stayed in their huts in the barracks, eating, drinking and fooling around, because this cost them nothing. A few had been drinking and amusing themselves so much that they had all but forgotten about God.

Some of the men built a little chapel from bamboo in which the cantors held services every Sunday and holy day. Afterwards, some kind of bearded parson came here, christened the children, served a mass and then left. Not having a priest of their own, the people conducted the religious activities themselves. One of the old cantors would place a large kerchief on his head, stand behind the altar and say mass, prayers for the dead (4) or perform other ceremonies. This went on for a long time. The immigration officials observed this closely and informed the government authorities who then stopped giving out supplies of food, saying: "Amuse yourselves now and be happy!"

The people began to protest and they demanded assistance. A dozen or so soldiers were called in who beat the protesters, including the old cantor who cried out, "Save yourselves, all those who believe in God!" Again the hunger and the poverty! Faced with the difficulties, the people became more serious about improving their fate and started collecting palm leaves, wild berries and mushrooms

Caboclos.

Бо справді на жінок у ті доби,
Ударили найгірші хороби.

for food. One family died from eating poisonous mushrooms. Only one of them survived. In desperation, some went to the Brazilians and begged for food.

The people did whatever they could to keep from starving. Some of the women even left their husbands and went to live with the Brazilian men, saying that at least they would be able to eat. Some of our boys also went to live with the Brazilians. They never returned home but became Brazilianized themselves. Living in such sad conditions, the people did not want to stay on their *shakry*. It came to such a point that the police had to force them to leave, throwing their possessions out of the huts and setting fire to the barracks.

Shortly after, the government built a beautiful chapel in Antônio Olinto. It was for the use of every nationality and the people would attend on Sundays and holy days. Without a priest, the cantors sang and conducted the services themselves. The haughty Poles, however, always put themselves before us and so their service would take place first. One time our people put a tetrapod inside but the Polish organist came and hid it from sight. When our elderly cantor, Ivan Hupalo, put it back in its place, the Pole snatched it from his hand and said "This is not a Greek Catholic church, it is a kościół" (5). There were arguments and struggles, some even leading to fist fights.

Because of this, the Ukrainians preferred to walk the 13 miles to Rio Claro for confession, for marriage ceremonies and other services. Father Rozdolsky served there for several years, having spent a short time in our colony before leaving for Rio Claro. He was truly our spiritual leader. Everything was in complete disorder when he left but then, quite unexpectedly, Father Martyniuk arrived and spent a longer time here. Hearing the word of God from this missionary, many people turned their lives around. The women who went over to the Brazilians now feared the wrath of God and many of them returned to their husbands. The Brazilians hated Martyniuk for doing this, so much so that he often had to take the long way back to his quarters in order to protect himself from assault. These were the days when church services were performed in the people's houses and it was not safe for him to be outside alone. A shot was even fired at one young missionary who travelled from Lapa to see us.

We lived amid such conditions for two years. We were looked down upon terribly by the Brazilians who judged and regarded us as the lowest of all. Among them were some daredevils who did with the people whatever they wanted. In hearing about a wedding one time, some of them caused such trouble that the guests ran and hid in the weeds. This did not last too long, though. As our boys got older, they began to fight back and the troublemakers left.

A Ukrainian Catholic church in Antônio Olinto, Paraná.

The next priest to serve here was Father Klymentiy Bzhukhovsky. The people complained to him bitterly that the Poles were disrespecting and degrading our people. Bzhukhovsky replied, "It is time for us to build our own chapel and then a church." In time, a house was also purchased where the visiting priests would stay. When Bzhukhovsky came a second time, a meeting was held where everyone agreed that it was necessary for us to build a church of our own. Almost immediately we bought the closest *shakra* to the city, cleared some of the forest and brought in a house which we had purchased.

Within a couple of days everything was ready. Half of the building was designated for the chapel and the other half as living quarters for the priest. We hung our pictures and banners from the community chapel and rejoiced in now having our own. Father Bzhukhovsky began visiting more often, especially when we started

Та Бог наслав на тую злюку бич,
Попавсь нам лепський русначок-панич.

work on the church. With the blessing of the cornerstone, the people cut down trees and moved heavy timbers. We owe a debt of gratitude to Father Bzhukhovsky and remain grateful to him until today for his help and guidance. We had the services of a carpenter from Rio Claro and within a few months the church was ready.

With the building of the church, we also founded the first church Brotherhood of Ivan Khrystytel and the first reading club. It was active for a few months but then ceased to function. No one knows what happened to all the books. The people also observed that another important institution, a school, was necessary. Father Bzhukhovsky called a meeting and described the importance of a school and education for the children. The people embraced the idea and immediately decided that one should be established. The first teacher was Mr. S. Duma. There was still no location for a schoolroom, with the chapel and the living quarters for the priest located in the house, and so Mr. Duma taught the children in his own home.

Duma was a simple farmer, just literate, but he was a sincere and honest man. He did considerable good for the community and always stood in the defence of our betterment and well-being. He advised, helped and taught everyone, all of us drawing from his knowledge and optimism. There were, for example, no primers for the students and so he would spend his evenings copying out lines from his book and preparing lessons for his students for the next day! He taught very well and his work produced real results. Many of his students remember him fondly and are grateful to this day. In addition to teaching, Duma was also the postmaster. He later handed the post office over to another man who, unfortunately, did not attend to it as he should have which caused a great deal of problems and misunderstandings. Duma lost a large sum of money over this and was forced to sell his land and leave the colony.

There were further changes when Father Mykhalchuk arrived and took the parish under his wing. The people purchased another building, an old house which became the priest's residence, and which provided a location for the school. Another two schools were later established, built by the people themselves. They functioned very well in the beginning but are now abandoned.

The church has been expanded considerably and is beautifully painted. Material is also being prepared for the construction of a new schoolhouse. We have had our own priest for 24 years already.

Free emigration to the state of Minas Gerais, Brazil was offered by the steamship line La Veloce of Genoa, Italy.

Списав він лист слізми облитий,
До їх там королеви Маргарити.

The beginnings of settlement.

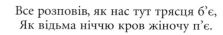

Все розповів, як нас тут трясця б'є,
Як відьма ніччю кров жіночу п'є.

Chapter 8
And for the Meal Pyrohy and Piranhas

Luca Morski

Luca Morski was born in 1866 in the village of Khmelyska, county Skalat, East Galicia, to his parents Teodor Morski and Varvara Oliynyk. He married Anna Khrushch and had two children, Mykola, born in 1892, and Katia, born in 1894. Luca and his family were among the first immigrants in Brazil, arriving in 1896 and settling near Prudentópolis, Paraná, in linha Cônsul Pohl. His wife Anna died in 1900. Later that year he married Varvara Hevchuk, native of the village of Kryve, Skalat county, who came to Brazil with her family in 1896. They had six children: Teodoro, Maria, Basílio, Pedro, João and Marta. In 1909, his first-cousin, Danylo Morski, emigrated to Paraná, settling alongside and bringing another branch of the family tree to Brazil. Luca Morski died on March 26, 1916.

There was much talk in our village about Brazil. The steamship agents, including Gergoletto (1), had visited many times and did a good job in promoting settlement across the sea. They told of all kinds of riches, free land for everyone and even streets paved with emeralds. The people listened. And they were captivated and curious about this new land.

Our neighbours, the Kravchuk, Serbai and Mamchur families, had already left for Brazil. Others were preparing to leave and were selling their land, possessions and farm animals. I too had decided to emigrate. My father did not understand my decision but he did not forbid me from going across the sea. He knew of the difficulties of life in the village, the shortage of land and the lack of opportunities for the younger generation. And after all, he said, I was a Morski. And now I would be living up to our family's name (2).

It was time to leave. The goodbyes lasted for three days. Those who had already come to see us off would come again. The women cried. They held on to each other, begged forgiveness for any past offences and cried some more. The men were more composed. The children did not understand the commotion and were excited about the adventure. Our priest, Father Verbytsky, and some of the older women said that they would pray for our safe arrival.

There were so many people leaving. Whole groups had departed previous to ours. What would become of our village?

We travelled by wagon to the train station in Skalat. Boarding the train, we arrived in Ternopil and then continued on to Lviv, our journey taking us through the cities of Stryi, Budapest, Rijeka (3), Gorizza–our checkpoint at the Italian border–Udine and then to Genoa where we would board the ship for Brazil. Some of the emigrants took a different route. Leaving Lviv, they would travel to Kraków, then Vienna, Villach and Pontebba before reaching Udine and continuing on to the port in Genoa. The trip lasted about four days. The train was searched at every stop as the gendarmes looked for military recruits, vagrants or other illegal passengers who might be trying to emigrate.

We arrived in Gorizza at the end of February 1896. It was here that we encountered the first of our problems. Although we had made arrangements to travel to the state of Paraná, we were informed that we would be going to Espírito Santo instead. The officials from the St. Raphael Society had told us not to change our plans and to go nowhere else other than Paraná. The people protested. There was yelling, shouting and calls for our plans to remain as they were. We wanted to emigrate to Paraná.

 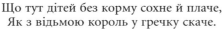

Що тут дітей без корму сохне й плаче,
Як з відьмою король у гречку скаче.

The farmstead of a Ukrainian family near Prudentópolis. In the centre and to the left, the ubiquitous pinheiros.

І помогло. Пустили нас якстій.
Урвалось поганій відьмі тій.

The situation worsened. The representatives of the steamship company would not honour our passage to Paraná and we would be sent back to Galicia if we did not go to Espírito Santo. The Italian authorities intervened and decided to force the whole transport to return. When the train pulled into the station, some of our women grabbed their children and threw themselves in front of the train, saying to the officials that they preferred death to returning to the homeland where they had lost everything.

We were sent on to Genoa–not back to Galicia–for further discussion. There was such confusion at the pier. The people did not know what to do nor what to expect and the situation was only made worse by the weeping of the women and children all around. What would happen to us? Would we be left behind watching the ships go by, as we say in Portuguese? (4) *Se Deus quiser*, we would make it to Paraná (5).

After some investigation, we discovered that we had been deceived. Duped. Our agent Nodari had prepared our travel documents directing us to Espírito Santo. It was only after long negotiations and much persuasion on our part that we were able to leave as planned, to Rio de Janeiro and then to Paraná. We heard later that the Italian authorities stepped in and began to further investigate Nodari and his activities.

We arrived in Rio de Janeiro in mid-March. It was a difficult crossing which lasted about three weeks. Free passage to Brazil had ended in [June] 1891. The prices of steamship tickets were 75 *mil reis* for adults and children over the age of 12. It was half this amount for children aged eight to 12 and a quarter for infants. I had saved enough money for tickets for the four of us and still had several hundred left over which would help us settle in. So many people died on board, especially the children. Prayers were said over their little bodies and they were tossed into the sea. Out of despair, one of the women attempted to jump overboard after her child and it was only because of the quick action of a sailor that she was saved.

We spent a long time at the barracks on Ilha das Flores. These were terrible times. The conditions were poor, there was a shortage of food and people were dying all around. There was a little boy who entertained us with his *sanfona* (6). Other Brazilians tempted us with food and items of clothing. One of the men wore a wide-brimmed straw hat on top of which he piled all of his wares. There were different kinds of fruits, onions, fish and a small rosy-coloured octopus, its arms hanging down and slapping the side of his face every time he moved his head. From Rio, we travelled by smaller steamship along the coast to Paranaguá and from there by train to Curitiba. Throughout these days we were bombarded by the great *fazendeiros* (7) who were trying to get workers for their plantations which had been standing empty since [the abolition of slavery in Brazil in] 1888.

Curitiba was an interesting city. It was so different from any of ours in Europe. We were told that Ukrainians had settled here as early as 1891. One of my father's friends, Mr. Pastukh and his family, had emigrated the year previous and we would be staying with him. He lived in Prudentópolis which was located further inland from Curitiba.

Luca Morski.

We travelled by train from Curitiba to the town of Ponta Grossa and then would continue on to Prudentópolis by *carroça*. We spent longer than we had planned in Ponta Grossa. It was difficult to manage with all of our possessions—trunks full of clothes, dishes, some tools. Katia was not feeling well and at times hardly had the

А як ми вже на корабель сідали,
То панича від нас арештували.

energy to walk. We did not know what was wrong. My wife had brought some different herbs from the old country and made some tea for her to drink. It seemed to help.

It was hard to get a *carroça*. With so many immigrants, the drivers were busy and we would have to wait for some time before leaving. The barracks were terrible. They were just little sheds for us to sleep in. We were given food but we had to prepare it for ourselves. In such filth and squalor it is a wonder that we did not become sick before ever reaching Prudentópolis.

Until I die I will never forget these first weeks in Brazil. I remember sitting under a shelter of palm leaves, the rain pouring down around us as we spent our first night in the jungle on the way to the city. I remember how glad I was to see father's friend! I remember the welcome he and his family extended. He took us to his home so we did not have to spend any time in the barracks. In the two years since he arrived, he managed to build a house, clear some land and even purchase a few animals. But this place was so different. Red soil, stifling heat, brightly coloured parrots. And for the meal *pyrohy* and piranhas.

After a few months we left our hosts in [the colony of] Nova Galícia. Land was being measured out in *linha* Cônsul Pohl, some six kilometres away where I would claim my *shakra*. These were land parcels of about 25 hectares, a quarter kilometre wide, a whole kilometre long and numbered in order. The area was covered with a thick forest of pinheiro, imbuia and bracatinga trees and it would take months of back-breaking work to clear even the smallest plot. The first years were very difficult and I do not know how we survived. The people even told about their hardships in a song—

> Oh, I know, I know my native Galicia.
> > But now I know this foreign land.
> All of our family lives in Galicia
> > While here in Brazil we have become poor.
> And so we came, but we did not find any gold.
> > We stand under the pinheiro and weep bitterly.
> There is nothing to eat here, only black beans,
> > And we abandoned our fields in Galicia.
> There are still no beans.
> > And it is 24 miles to walk to work.
> Mate tea for breakfast and sweet potatoes for lunch
> > But you're not called to the house for supper.

The train station in Skalat.

I quickly learned the method of clearing the land here. The thick undergrowth was hacked away with a *foice* and *facão* (8). The larger trees were cut with saws. It was very dangerous when felling trees, especially the pinheiros which were so large that it often took the work of several men to cut through just one tree. Another danger was the dry cones, as big as pumpkins, which would come lose and fall to the ground. One of the settlers was killed when a cone was shaken loose and fell on his head. The stumps were then burned and you were left with a clean piece of land.

A small hut had already been built on my *shakra* and so our efforts were first put into clearing some land for a field. We planted potatoes, the Brazilian *batatas* (sweet potatoes) and *mandioca*. In time, we also cleared and planted a vegetable garden and an orchard of orange and banana trees. I planted some coffee saplings which were given to me by one of the settlers. Beans were cultivated in between the rows.

Life in the colonies was not easy. Everything was so different from what it had been in Europe. There were ants, the number and size of which I had never seen before. They would destroy seed grain, vegetable gardens and the fruit of entire orchards. Locusts and worms, though not appearing every year, made for further damage. Care had to be taken in the dense forest while clearing land. There were poisonous

Немов би то він ошуканець єсть...
Він нам шепнув—«Се злої відьми месть!»

snakes and spiders whose bites caused the death of many settlers since antidotes were not readily available. The intense summer heat would scorch the crops during the day, while heavy frosts froze them at night. There was often a lack of proper fodder for the cattle and they suffered terribly from fleas.

We learned many lessons from trial and error. Some vegetables were very susceptible to the Brazilian frosts and could only be planted in spring, that is in September or October. Lime juice was an effective treatment for diphtheria. Hard woods, such as bracatinga, produced the best wood ash for making soap and fertilizer. Soft woods, such as imbuia and pinheiro, produced ash with a lesser percentage of potash and phosphorus. Fleas on cattle could be treated with vinegar in which orange peels had been soaked or with the water in which potatoes were boiled, both of which were applied to the animals topically.

My wife Anna died in 1900 and I remarried later that same year. In 1908, my daughter Katia died of typhus at the age of 14. She had been weak for some time but we did not know Portuguese and were unable to speak with a doctor. Some of the women tried to help her but she grew weaker and weaker. She was buried next to her mother in the cemetery in Cônsul Pohl.

Three generations in Brazil. Luca Morski's son Mykola Morski (right), his grandson João Morski (standing second from left) and great-grandsons Antônio and Daniel Morskei (seated).

«Мовчіть, бо пропадете всі дочиста!»
Ми—ша! Пропало наших ринських триста.

Galician passport of Ivan Hevchuk, native of the village of Kryve, Skalat county, who emigrated to Brazil in 1896.

По морі ми плили без злих пригод.
Лиш хорував погано ввесь народ.

Chapter 9: Among Our People in South America

Petro Karmansky

Petro Karmansky (1878-1956) first travelled to Brazil in 1919, a date which marked the beginning of his complex and controversial association with the Ukrainian community there. He was a delegate from the Western Ukrainian National Republic and visited Brazil and Argentina in order to solicit financial support for the struggle for independence in the homeland. Karmansky left Brazil in 1922 but returned later that same year to Prudentópolis where he was engaged by the Basilian Order as the editor of their newspaper *Prácia*. Conflicts soon arose. Karmansky was critical of the Basilians and their work in Brazil and was discharged from the newspaper. In 1924 he established a rival publication, *Khliborob*. The ensuing polemical action against him, known as *Karmanshchyna*, led to the publication of his book *Chomu? (Why?)* in 1925 in an attempt to vindicate himself and his work among the Ukrainians in Brazil.

In spite of the problems, Karmansky made numerous contributions within the Ukrainian-Brazilian community, most notably in the areas of culture and education. A Ukrainian college was established in Brazil in 1926 as a result of his efforts. As a writer, he is regarded as the first to introduce Brazilian elements into Ukrainian literature.

The following are excerpts from his *Mizh ridnymy v Pivdennii Amerytsi (Among Our People in South America)* in which he describes his visit to the Ukrainian settlements of Brazil in 1922, more than 30 years after the arrival of the first immigrants.

FEBRUARY 28, BETWEEN IRATÍ AND PRUDENTÓPOLIS

Twenty-eight hours travelling by train—through endless forests, mountain valleys of wild grasses waving in the wind, and more forests. At every glance you see the graceful pinheiros (Brazilian pines) with curved branches resembling parasols which produce piles of hard, wide and prickly needles. Among them, the proud palm trees, impassable thickets of bamboo, erva mate (Brazilian tea), wild ferns and all types of bushes and flowers which I had previously known only from the botanical gardens. There are tall fields of corn, grapes, orange trees with their still dark-green fruit and other trees and flowers which, despite my knowledge of botany, I cannot identify. The train winds like a snake along a narrow, red-coloured path... Hill after hill, to the right, to the left. And forest all around—pinheiros and palms.

A hundred or so kilometres still remains before we reach the last station but our journey would be taking a break. We will continue on tomorrow.

I stopped in the town of Ponta Grossa and stayed at the Hotel Santos, the proprietors of which were Negroes. In the evening I went to see their small-town *Carnaval* (1), an event which has accompanied me on this whole trip as even passengers, mainly children, board the trains dressed in costume and makeup. I listened to the strange and whimsical music and then left early the next morning, all with the precision of a machine.

I finally arrived in Iratí from where I would be continuing on by horse and wagon. Some young boys carried my baggage to the home of the Ukrainian shopkeeper, a man from Ternopil county, where I saw that my wagon was already there and waiting.

My host took this time to tell me a little about himself. He told how he came to Brazil 25 years ago with the first transport of emigrants, how the people suffered for two months in Udine in Italy, how everyday a few more were counted and sent off at the landing pier in Brazil and how they lived in

На морі вмерло дев'ять душ народу.
Їх замість погребу метали в воду.

the palm-covered barracks in the middle of the endless forests of Paraná. My stories about the misery in the homeland did not interest him, he said. He had not seen the problems and did not know anything about them. He asked only how much money you would have in Galicia for so many thousand *mil reis*. I had lunch with him, eating *kapusniak* (2) and some wonderful fried chicken, for which I paid two *mil reis*, and continued on my way. I climbed on the wagon which was covered by a sackcloth roof and hitched to two pairs of horses whose bells jingled like alpine cattle. The road was slippery from the rain, dark red clay stuck to the wheels, the sun baked down and it looked like rain again.

Six hours of travelling on roads the likes of which were never seen back home. Hills, potholes, puddles, winding corners. It appeared that everything I had just eaten would be lost and that I would arrive at my destination completely cleansed. This was a very interesting road!

MY FRIEND OLEKSA!

It is impossible for me not to be thinking of you at this moment, my friend from those carefree days in the Vienna woods, who rejoiced when he saw the forest of green trees and did not hear the noise of the streetcars, who always dreamed of the peacefulness within the silence of the forests and of the deep and contemplative life of the philosopher Tagore. That, for which you have longed for years, I have right now. Boundless forests, narrow roads bordered by bamboo and wild bushes known to us only from the Scheinbrun Conservatory of tropical flowers, the graceful parasols of the pinheiros and the fluffy green tops of the palm trees. Hundreds of multicoloured butterflies and unfamiliar birds accompany me at every step; every few hours I come upon the saws for cutting the enormous pinheiros and two or three yellowish, curly-headed Brazilians with slanting eyes, on horseback, looking out from under wide-brimmed hats and raising their hand to extend the greeting "Bom dia" (3). Such is the culture of the people here! In the middle of this endless sea of green, in this dark and secluded corner of the forest, I am alone with my driver, a German from Austria, who has come to understand the world amidst this ocean of forest.

I do not know how you would feel if you were here in my place—and I am not able to tell you a lot about my own feelings. I dream, I dream and I lose myself in my dreams in these eternal forests of the Brazilian backwoods.

We stopped here for the night, having travelled half of the way, at a lone house which serves as an inn for travellers and a store for the local residents who are scattered about in this labyrinth of forest.

Home of the Sestry Sluzhebnytsi (Sisters Servants) in Dorizon, Paraná.

My driver unhitched the horses, weary from the trip, and took them to the forest to rest and I, having eaten dinner and drinking the fragrant mate tea, sat on the stoop of the house and mused. A monotone whistling sound of crickets comes from the forest darkness, here and there are flashes of light from the glow worm—and beyond that there is silence all around, lulling you to sleep with the peaceful rustling of the pinheiros and palms. What a terrible silence, what a beautiful silence!...

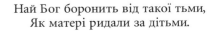

Най Бог боронить від такої тьми,
Як матері ридали за дітьми.

My friend! Why are you not here with me? Why are we not here together, helping each other to discover the soul of this ocean of forest? I have been searching for it for several days already, I feel it, I go to it but I am still unable to find it. I am a lost and little downcast traveller! I bow my head before our people who some 20 years ago were dropped as little specks of dust into this forested wilderness, cutting out from it a little window of sunlight, sowing corn and raising hogs and for whole months not seeing another human face. Such homesickness they must have had for their native villages all these long years! How I would love to go to each and every person, reciting for them our great history and bringing a little ray of light into their hearts which have been closed to all of life's pleasures for so long! These are futile wishes. In front of me stand the impassable walls of wild forest in which all difficulty awaits. I too am like a little speck of dust which the green ocean has seized and swallowed. I feel that I myself am dying for you, my sad friend, that at this moment you are chewing over the ideas of Tagore in some corner of a coffee house and longing for my solitude, while I ache for a cultured life and long for my past. Do you realize how far away I am from you and how far I have travelled from the bustling life of the capital? I am three days from the closest real city and only tomorrow will I reach my destination. And where will the near future lead me? How much further must I still travel through these woods of Sahara-like proportions with their wild life forms and their dangers? I am beginning to understand what naive children we were when we all sat in Vienna with a glass of wine, talking about Brazil and making plans for our future work in this country. Still whole generations of giants would have to go through this wilderness for us well-bred dreamers to pave a path to the heart of Brazil.

Brrr! such a terrible rustle of the forest, these backwoods have such an awful sound! I feel so vulnerable at this moment that I nervously grasp my revolver with my hand when I see the owner of the house with his dark eyes, his thin, black beard and his wide-brimmed hat!

It is beginning to rain. The whistle of the crickets echoes in my ears. The forest is falling asleep. The silence lulls me to sleep too and I feel like I could sleep like I haven't slept for years. I feel myself calming down. I feel my whole past slipping further and further away from me. Perhaps I truly will find here that for which I have been searching for so long. Goodnight, my friend, my unfortunate friend who is being eaten up by the prison of the coffee house! If I could only give you a little of this huge ocean of forest! I am drowning in it and I am losing myself here. I fear that I am quickly disappearing from you, my friends, those closest to me. Oh, if you only knew what blessings the telegraph, post office and railroad are! I have lost these long, long ago. Goodnight.

PRUDENTÓPOLIS, MARCH 3

This is already my third day at the monastery of the Basilian Fathers and I am sitting in my spacious attic room and looking out of the open window at the "city." Little

Monastery of the Basilian Fathers in Iracema, Santa Catarina.

 Коли їх риби довгі мов ті бальки,
Зубаті, чорні, рвали на кавалки!

houses are located on even clearings in the middle of the forest—in disorder and disarray. Here and there are gardens planted with corn and erva mate, the main source of income for our settlers. A wonderful new pavilion, the monastery of the Basilian Fathers, is located on the hill abreast of which stands our Ukrainian church, flanked with palms, and a nice National Home with the trident symbol. Over there is the Polish Roman Catholic church and the municipal school which stands empty because the children, both Ukrainian and Polish, study in private schools (the school run by the Sisters Servants has an enrolment of some 200 children) and other buildings. The city has a population of 8,000 people but they are all spread out in the forest in an area of several square miles. This is the largest Ukrainian settlement. Elections for their political leader were held on the very day of my arrival with their candidate winning by a majority of 170 votes. The Basilian Fathers rejoiced like children and the Ukrainians shot off their guns all night long in celebration. I observed this childlike mirth and, for them, the intoxicating victory but I was unable to understand the reason for such rejoicing. I was, nonetheless, touched by their national consciousness and how much concern and value they placed in their own issues. I looked with silent respect at these three men in their white cassocks. Their influence had reached the furthest corners of the Paraná forests as they hardly had a moment to descend from their mules, covering miles and miles of roads and impassable trails. Father Kotsylovsky himself travels by mule. He will cover eight miles today and then return home in three weeks. He has almost drowned twice already and several times nearly met his death by falling off his mule. But in spite of this he is always happy, smiling and enthusiastic about his work.

This gives me such a strange feeling! I look at the old men in the church, stooped with age, with their typical Ukrainian faces and thick mustaches, and at the old women, with kerchiefs on their heads and dressed as if they just yesterday arrived from Galicia and it is hard to believe that these people have been living in these Brazilian backwoods for several years already. Their children and grandchildren, also dressed in traditional Galician clothing, play on the wide streets, speaking Ukrainian, reading from the prayer books in church and growing up to be Ukrainians themselves.

I sit in my comfortable room, I look out at the neat little houses set about the green orchards and at the parasols of pinheiros which surround the city from all sides, I listen to the choir singing inside the church and to the conversations of the old men on the street and this brings about a strange sensation. Where am I? In our Galician village or among the endless forests of Paraná? And this creates within me the faith in the immortality of our people and the hope for our future. I hear even young Brazilian children from mixed marriages speaking Ukrainian and many of the older Brazilians speak our language no worse than any one of us. Is this not a sign of our culture and strength?

MARCH 5

Grey clouds hang fixed in the sky. It looks like rain. The roosters are crowing without stop, calling for good weather.

Our first meeting was held today at which I read a paper about our liberating movement. Several hundred settlers from Prudentópolis and other locales gathered at the large hall of the Ukrainian National Home—men, women, boys and girls. They sat huddled together on benches, men on the left, women on the right. It was lovely to look at.

I spoke, telling the people what Galicia has endured for these last seven years, what it is facing presently and what it can expect for the future. Everyone listened intently as tears rolled down their faces. My speech lasted almost two hours but no one made a move even though they were tired from the church service and it was already long past the time for the midday meal. No one interrupted with a word, no one coughed, no one made the smallest motion. They listened to me as if they were listening to the very grieving of their native, blood-stained land, as a son would listen to his father who had returned from a distant country after years of absence. I looked into these familiar faces, etched with years of grief and sorrow, I looked into their gentle eyes filled with tears and my voice became stuck in my throat. I had to stop my sad story. I saw before me a Ukrainian spirit which is still very much alive. I saw the sons of Ukraine who after all these years in this forested wilderness are still dreaming the Ukrainian dream, rejoicing and suffering with their homeland. I saw these same men, some two years ago leaving their native land, and know that neither climate nor strange surroundings nor different lifestyle had changed them... The new generation is growing up in the same way, coming into the world under the Brazilian sun and regarding themselves as Brazilian citizens. The Ukrainian soul is nourished by the Sisters Servants who, alongside Portuguese, teach Ukrainian in the schools and even keep alive the unique Ukrainian chauvinism.

В Бразилії теж зазнали зла,
Пропасниця лиха на нас зайшла.

It is funny to me! I look out the window at the groves of erva mate and at the gardens of mandioca and grapes and corn, my eyes wander upwards above the parasol-like pinheiros and the drooping fluffy green palms and I hear the sound of the children's choir in school singing *Shche ne vmerla* (4). I feel like I am in a dream because it is only there that such contrasts could exist. But this is not a dream. And I am not sleeping!

PORTO UNIÃO, MARCH 21

I am again in a different house. My host from Porto União mounts his horse and rides several miles in the rain to tell some of the more well-to-do locals about my arrival. A group gathered after lunch where we drank vermouth and then went for a lovely evening meal at a wonderful restaurant. The conversation lasted until almost midnight when one of the more affluent men, the proprietor of a modern haberdashery and married to a German woman who speaks Ukrainian rather well, took me to his house, some four kilometres away, where I am accommodated in a comfortable room.

P.S. I am sitting over a gasosa (lemonade) in the store of one of our settlers and am surrounded by a myriad of interesting sights and sounds. In the neighbouring room a parrot is shouting with all its might in Ukrainian, "Mykola, give the parrot some peas" or is chiding the proprietress, saying, "Where did you go?" and then again warbles some Ukrainian melodies. And no one pays any attention to this because it is all seen as something quite natural. Our settlers have adapted themselves to the new way of life and worry how difficult it would be for them to get used once again to the old ways of the homeland. They also worry about their children becoming Brazilianized and that they do not understand their parents and already are not feeling connected to our life. Be that as it may, it is necessary to note that denationalization does not affect our younger Brazilian generation to the same degree that it does the children of the other [immigrant] settlers.

My host's father-in-law is a German from Prussia and his wife is a German woman who was born in Brazil. Their young children (there are seven of them) speak to their father only in Ukrainian and to their grandfather in perfect Portuguese. Their mother speaks to them in Ukrainian no worse than any one of our Paraskas! Compare this with mixed marriages in Galicia or Ukraine... You look at everything and you are awed and amazed. Give them a good school and our Brazilian-Ukrainians will make miracles.

PONTA GROSSA, APRIL 14

After a seven-hour train ride I stopped in a town similar in size to our Zolochiv, second in size after Curitiba in the state of Paraná. It is spread out on a hill in the middle of these boundless backwoods, these treeless campos resembling the Canadian prairies (5).

I am sitting in a clean enough hotel, the proprietor of which is a Negro, and I am listening to the noise of the large crowd which has gathered outside on the church grounds. This was Good Friday, a great holy day in Brazil. And while not one of the factories blew its whistle for the entire day, nor did the train which went from morning to sunset without announcing its arrival, an orchestra is now playing a mournful march by the church.

I sit, I listen to the noise of the crowd, I hear the music and I am feeling bitter. This is already my fourth Easter in a row away from home. In Switzerland, in Rome,

A Ukrainian Catholic church near Prudentópolis.

 Три місяці чекали ми на Квіти,
Три хлопи вмерли тут і три кобіти.

Vienna and now here in the Brazilian forests. But I have my own native land, my own family and my own beloved children!

Today is April 14. Spring is awakening on the other side of the ocean, the orchards are starting to turn green, the trees are beginning to adorn themselves with flowers. Nature here, it seems, is starting to wane, the flowers are finished blooming, the sun bakes down during the day and you can feel the bite of cold after it sets. Winter will begin in a week or two... Outside of the windows the sound of the celebrating crowd and the music of the mournful march continue. Christ is Risen!

APRIL 16

It is four o'clock in the morning. At the little church the women have set down their *pasky* (6), fireworks are set off, the children are making a joyful chatter and the place is full of people.

The Easter procession makes its way out of the church, the banners are rustling, candles are burning and sounding through the twilight is the old and powerful song "Christ is Risen!" The bells ring. The procession around the church begins and it is almost as if some secret power has transported this whole throng of people across the ocean, across ten different countries to their Galician village; how easy it is to forget that your feet are standing on Brazilian soil and that this early morning chilliness is not that of the end of winter but of the beginning. How strange it is that beside these mothers and their *pasky* the children are chattering in Portuguese and you want to believe that it is only an echo of a sound from somewhere else.

A group of girls, boys and children gathered around the church. The bells are ringing, fireworks explode in the air, songs are sung and the smiles of carefree faces are everywhere. *Yide, yide Zelman*—the song resounds, the girls performing the round dance for the crowd of boys and children (7). Everyone—those who still speak Ukrainian today and those who have already taken this foreign language as their own—is singing and has found for a moment the forgotten treasure of our native song and our native spirit, all coming together into one Ukrainian family, everyone's hearts filled with warmth and gladness. This miracle will continue as long as the Easter holidays keep bringing them to their native church, as long as they do not lose their native songs in this foreign land and as long as the Easter and Christmas celebrations fill their souls with this great love and respect which only the soul of the Ukrainian people knows.

MAY 5

A speaking platform was built amidst the branches of the giant imbuia tree, as it is done here in the backlands, and was surrounded by several hundred listeners, of all ages and of both sexes, forming a wonderful image on the green background. From minute to minute there was the noise of mortars being discharged, creating a rumble through the endless forest.

The meeting began after a solemn church service for those who had fallen. The sad stories about the difficulties in the Galician homeland were told from the platform set under the outstretched branches of the imbuia. So much poetry in such a meeting, so much beauty in such a country! Women and some of the men, the old, long-haired elders, wiped their tears with hands hardened from years of work. I myself am barely able to keep back the tears which have welled in my eyes. The stories end and the song begins to echo through these backwoods: *Shche ne vmerla! Ne pora!* (8) The long and exhausting trip across the ocean has been worth the experience of moments such as these.

Our unfortunate settlers pull out their last *mil reis* from their small bundles and give the money as donations to help the homeland. One villager gave the amount of 500 *mil reis*... And I can hardly keep myself from crying out: keep them for yourselves and your children, these wrinkled and damp bank notes, you yourselves are poor, so poor! A little old woman, a widow, her hand trembling from age, came up at the end and gave a silver *mil reis*. Within a half-hour the total had reached nearly 3,000.

How can you not love these people?... Poverty drove them across the sea 27 years ago, especially the young people whose national consciousness had not yet been awakened. There were years of terrible suffering and misfortune. Among the isolated forested backlands, among strangers and wild Indians, they grew up and silently wept for their native villages. Now after several years of life in bitter isolation, they reminisce to one another about their villages, saying that they still remember every path and often see their native houses in their dreams as if it were just yesterday that they had left them behind. And although today the trees have been cleared by their hard work, although there are now many miles of roads which they cut through the forests, although orange trees glimmer and flower gardens smile by their houses and although many of those former old country labourers are now prosperous landowners—at the same time they all bemoan their long suffering and pray to this very moment that they be taken back to their native shore.

 П'ять хлопців до услуг продали ми,
А цім дівчат пішли в такі доми.

Chapter 10 | We Cooked the Chicken Seven Times

Luca Morski

> Luca Morski's memoirs continue with the story of his goddaughter's wedding in 1904. In spite of the string of small disasters which marked their wedding day, Ana Kravchuk and João Paulo Lypka were married and lived happily ever after. Regrettably the story was left unfinished. Where did the wedding take place? Was there a similar celebration at the home of the groom's family? Did Hryts, the musician, really break his nose? The fate of the chicken also remains unknown.

Who could forget Ana's wedding? What fuss, what commotion! Such *bagunça*! (1) And yet the day had started off so calmly! When Ana announced that she was getting married to João Paulo Lypka, it was a cause for celebration. He was a nice young man, handsome and tall as a pinheiro. [My wife] Varvara and I were invited to the house to help with the plans. I was Ana's godfather and was asked to play the role of the *starosta* (2). I was honoured and, of course, accepted immediately.

The day had arrived. Early on Friday morning we began setting up the tables and benches outside on the yard. Some of the men fashioned a large umbrella out of palm branches to shade the musicians as they played. Mr. Makush would be bringing his *tsymbaly* (3). It was a beautiful day. Hot but not too hot. Breezy but not too breezy. The sky was bright and sunny with a few clouds hanging in the distance.

Inside the house the women were tending to the food. Bean-filled *pyrohy*, *holubtsi*, sweet potatoes, *borshch* and a fat young chicken would be served to the first of the guests. The girls were piling oranges and bananas onto plates and placing them on each of the tables. Mrs. Kravchuk was washing dishes and had already broken two saucers. Two of the women were fussing with the chicken, setting it into a large iron pot and putting it back into the bake-oven. This was the second time they had done this. The oven had not been heated sufficiently and the chicken still needed to cook.

The guests began arriving by mid-afternoon. The musicians started to play their lively songs and everyone was happy. There was so much noise, so much chatter and the always present sound of the clapping of hands. Some of the food was being served and bottles of *pinga* (4) were set on the table. Then it happened. There was the sound of thunder in the distance and a large black cloud rolled in and the rain poured down. Everyone scurried for cover. The women grabbed the food and took it back into the house. Pots were set to reheat, the chicken was put back in the oven and the water was drained from the plates of fruit.

The rain did not last very long and soon after the party continued on. The musicians played, some of the girls were dancing and the women passed the food through the window of the house to the hungry guests outside. The rain had caused one other problem. It leaked into the oven and extinguished the coals. The chicken was still undercooked. Mrs. Kravchuk blamed her husband for not patching the oven walls. Mr. Kravchuk reminded his wife that her mother was not a very good cook either. The poor chicken, still pale and lukewarm, went back into the oven.

 Про хлопців досі ми не мали вісти,
Дівчата раді, є що пити і їсти.

Some time had passed. More guests arrived, others had found a shady spot to rest and plates of food had been refilled. The chicken had just made an appearance when two of the men started to argue. One of them had fallen in the mud which caused the former to laugh and the latter to be terribly offended. A fight broke out and by the time the conflict had been resolved the food was cold and everything was taken back inside to reheat. Everyone laughed, saying that this was the fifth trip to the oven for Mrs. Kravchuk's chicken.

Many of the wedding traditions were observed. Ana's father made sure of this. There was the plaiting of the wreaths, the offering of the *korovai* (5), which had been baked with wheat flour for this special occasion, and her brothers saw to it that João Paulo would pay them an appropriate ransom. [In this ritual] he was barred from coming to the home of Ana's parents by her male relatives. He would first have to pay them a few *cruzeiros* (6). A second barrier, the men brandishing wooden sticks for swords, was set up before the house where he had to convince them to let him through and pay another ransom. It was a delight to watch. Of course the men decided to do this just as the tables had been set with food. Everything was cold and would have to be heated again.

Hryts, one of the musicians from Mamborê, had too much to drink and fell off the chair into the mud. Such yelling, such crying! It appeared he had broken his nose. Everything was stopped for the moment to help him. One of the older women suggested placing a banana peel over his nose. It was cool and moist and would prevent any swelling. The food! The pots and plates of *pyrohy*, *holubtsi*, sausages—and the chicken—were left untouched during Hryts's minor accident and had cooled again.

There would be at least one more trip to the kitchen.

Wedding of Andrukh Peretiatko and Zosia Bezushko, Barabonita.
Top row left: João Morski, Galician-born son of pioneer settlers in linha Cônsul Pohl.

Тут по лісах блукають дикі люди,
Б'ють наших і їдять. І нам мабуть то буде.

Chapter 11: Letters Home
Pedro Veltchevski, Fedorko Mechalovsky, João Petrovitch

> Amid the articles and editorials about the Ukrainian emigration to Brazil in the 1890s, the Ukrainian press printed some of the letters which the settlers wrote to their family and friends back home. As in Lviv's *Batkivshchyna*, they were published by the newspaper's editors as warnings for those still planning to emigrate to Brazil. Other newspapers published them as a means of informing their readership about the Ukrainian-Brazilian settlements. In all cases they preserve and provide valuable information about pioneer life.
>
> The first two letters, written by Veltchevski and Mechalovsky, appeared in *Batkivshchyna* in 1891 and 1896, respectively. The letter from Petrovitch, a native of the village of Horodyshche, county Sokal, was originally sent to his parish priest, Father Antin Bonchevsky, and printed in Lviv's *Svoboda* in 1898.

RIO CARULIN, FEBRUARY 9, 1891
MY DEAR OSYP (1)!

May the first words of this letter to you be "Glory to Jesus Christ." It is by the grace of God that we are safe and sound, and we hope you are the same, though we have not been spared tragedy. Our youngest son, Oleksa, died after our arrival.

Here is what we can tell you about our trip. It is not true that you will be refunded your money in Brazil like the people say. It is all a fraud. We did not have to purchase steamship tickets but travelled to Bremen at our own cost where a German man took us to the ship and we sailed at the expense of the government. I had 100 or so rubles which was sufficient for us. We sailed for 18 days before arriving in Brazil. From our point of entry we travelled for another two days to a second station and from there another day by ship before arriving in the colony.

My God! How terrible this was! They said that we would be living in colonies with houses and supplies but this was nothing more than a wild frontier without any protection. There is a new government in Brazil and it wants to settle these frontier areas. We were told to cut down trees and build huts but how could a poor man cope in such a wasteland full of snakes and wild animals! We have suffered a great misfortune and we now see what has happened to us for believing in those stories.

Our fellow Europeans knew better about life in Brazil. They did not want to settle here and so agents were sent all the way to our country where they found us stupid peasants who believed the fables and followed them like sheep to the slaughter. Oh God, how can we escape from this hellish place and return to our beloved Galicia?! It will not be easy. Brazil is surrounded by the sea and the trip [home] costs more than 100 rubles per person. My heart aches that we did not say our proper goodbyes, that we rushed so frantically to our departure and sold our possessions for half of their value. All of my hard work has been for the profit of others.

We are very sad living here amongst these foreigners. We cannot speak to them because we do not know their language. There are no churches, no priests, and we hear neither our native language nor our songs.

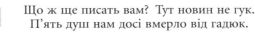

Що ж ще писати вам? Тут новин не гук.
П'ять душ нам досі вмерло від гадюк.

A view of Prudentópolis, 1911. Far left, the first Ukrainian Catholic chapel of São Basílio, built in 1897. Middle and above, the first Ukrainian Catholic church, also of São Basílio, begun in 1901 and inaugurated in 1904.

Та може дасть нам Бог піднятися.
Було на сорок—є ще вісімнадцять.

I wish from the bottom of my heart that God grants us the means to return to our homeland and to see you all again. It will probably be Easter by the time you receive this letter. Oh God! You will be rejoicing on this great day while we poor souls will be crying tears. We are so abandoned that we do not even know when it is a holy day and when it is a regular week day.

Goodbye to you all. Please write soon.

CURITIBA, DECEMBER 1, 1895
MY DEAREST FAMILY!

I am writing to tell you that I arrived safely in Brazil, in the province [sic] of Paraná, on November 2 after travelling a full five weeks (2). I went as far as the city of Curitiba. My companions continued on to the city of Rio de Janeiro where they will receive their allotment of forested land in sections a quarter-kilometre wide and a whole kilometre long (3). They will have to cut down trees and clear this land before they can begin farming.

I beg each and every one of you, my brothers, not to emigrate to Brazil because you will only perish here in vain. My saving grace was that I did not bring my wife with me because she would not have survived. It is unbearably hot here during the day but cold at night. A third of the passengers died en route before we arrived in Brazil. Of those from our village, Kovalchuk's youngest daughter did not survive the trip. I have lost track of the rest.

I found a job working on the [building of the] railroad and pray to God that I will have the strength to return home to the village. My plight is very sad. Please forgive me, my dear family, for leaving you. The cruel world has taught me a hard lesson.

And you, my wife, do not cry for me. If God grants me the means to return, I will leave Brazil in May or June.

Here in Brazil I earn three *mil reis* (about two *zoloti rynski*) a day. Food and lodgings cost me two *mil reis* a day and so one is all I can save. When it rains, and sometimes the rain lasts for a whole month, all work stops and your savings are lost.

PRUDENTÓPOLIS, MARCH 27, 1898
DEAR FATHER!

I, a man downcast and miserable, send you greetings and heartfelt wishes for luck and good health. Thank you for asking about our fate here across the sea, we children of Ukraine, so scattered about the world.

We left behind the Ukrainian soil which was worked by our grandfathers, great-grandfathers and our fathers. We left behind the well-trodden roads and paths, our homes and hearths and our schools. We left our places of worship, all of which were built for our salvation, those church bells which awakened and called us to prayer, our priest who spoke to us the word of God and our native customs and traditions… It was God's will.

On one hand it is sad and distressing. Just like a mother who is separated from her child, she longs for him but becomes accustomed to his absence. So do we here in this eternal Brazilian wilderness. It is difficult to adjust, difficult to forget. Perhaps one day we will be rewarded with some joy and happiness for our suffering in beginning a new life in this country.

Descendants of some of the first pioneers.

 Одно лиш жаль, що вже по-руськи тут,
Молиться ні балакать не дадуть.

A fragment of one of the letters home.

Ours was a magnificent Babylon but we were forced to leave because there was no one from whom to learn nor to take an example. Everywhere, as they say, "As is the lord, so is the feast." Many people read but many were deluded.

This is our fate in Brazil. That which we lacked in the old country—forest and land—we now have. But there is so much work. Nothing was ready for us. Nothing.

Not many knew why they came. We had not been so clever after all… but knew only that we could not continue to live in our native land and had to flee beyond the sea. Our fate? We cannot say that it is a bad one because then we would risk offending God. We arrived at Paranaguá at our own cost. We were detained for awhile, given provisions and then another voyage. No one died of hunger. They gave us forest. No one asked if we had any money. No one lost his freedom under the will of others as can happen here. God had not abandoned us. He sent us a true shepherd, our priest, who brings His word to us in these eternal forests. He struggles and works for our salvation. He speaks and a man's heart is filled with gladness.

Deceived is the man who was promised shiny hills of gold across the sea, to be dug up and shovelled into bags, *pyrohy* ready and waiting to be eaten or other such luxuries. He did not know what or how this all happened when he arrived. Gold and sterling coins were exchanged for bread because he did not want to work. There was no way to return to Galicia. Many parents weep over the graves of their children and children weep over those of their parents.

I can also tell you that of the four families from the parish who travelled to Brazil, we are all alive except for one, Vasyl Moroz.

I end these few words and beg your kindness in reading this letter from a most unworthy servant and granting the favour of your reply.

На нас у місті крикнув Кандзюбиньскі—
"Nie wolno tutaj gadać po rusiński."

Chapter 12 | TO FIND MY FATHER

Paulo Muzêka

> Paulo Muzêka (Pavlo Muzyka) was born in the village of Koropets, Zolochiv county, East Galicia. Though intending to emigrate to Brazil with his family, he was detained on suspicion of not having completed his military service which was compulsory at that time for all Austrian males 18 years and older. In fact, Muzêka had not served his two years in the army and was prevented from leaving. His father, having sold his house, land, possessions, and with steamship tickets previously purchased, left for Brazil as planned. Although Muzêka succeeded in emigrating at a later date, it would be several years before he would see his father again.
>
> Like Kobrên, Muzêka wrote his memoirs on the occasion of the fortieth anniversary of the Ukrainian immigration in Brazil. His story was published in *Prácia* May-June 1936.

It was because of my family's situation that I left for Brazil. My *babunia* (1) died on St. Andrew's Day when I was 12 years old. My brother-in-law, whom my father had so accepted into our family, died that same year during Great Lent, leaving behind a wife and child. My mother died on the very day of the Feast of the Assumption of the Blessed Virgin (2). We were five children left without a mother. We managed like this for six years but when my sister got married and left home, it was even more difficult for us without a woman in the house. Father remarried shortly after.

My father always dreamed about improving his fate. He had only a half-*morg* of garden in the village but 14 *morgs* of field located further away where he decided to build a new house. Our well was located there too—some three kilometres from home—and it was difficult to transport water, especially in the winter. After much thought, and on the advice of our stepmother, we moved to the field, selling the garden in the village and building a new house. It was good in summertime. Everything was so close to the house. But it was terrible in winter.

Things were not going well at home. Our stepmother had no real interest in us, her stepchildren, nor did we in her which gave our father a lot of problems and unpleasantness. My brother Vasyl, seeing that he would not be able to continue living at home, went out and found work. The other children did too.

I learned afterwards that Vasyl was planning to leave for Brazil. I went to see him to find out more about his plans. He was almost ready to leave. He had no problems at all because he was travelling with his employer who was paying for his passage. When he and his family left, Vasyl left with them.

I was also interested in going to Brazil but it would not be as easy for me. My father agreed to sell his property to his brother for 1,500 *zoloti rynski* in order to raise the money for the trip. We would all leave for Brazil. In the end, however, my uncle refused to hold up his end of the agreement because land prices had started to fall. They finally agreed on a price of 700. Our land was not of the best quality. There were sloughs from Zolochiv to the east and such clay that oats would not even grow there.

At that time, as with everyone who had reached the age of 20, I was required to go the army. I was to report in October. Plans, however, had now changed. Everything was packed and loaded on the wagons in preparation for our departure... There

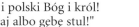

"Tu polski kraj i polski Bóg i król!
Po polsku gadaj albo gębę stul!"

A community's welcome for a visiting Ukrainian Catholic priest (seated, front left), near Prudentópolis.

 Га, що ж, коли так острий ферлядунок,
Хай буде й так! Який нам тут ратунок?

were a lot of us and it was crowded. The youngest was crying... I walked behind and then caught up to the wagon and jumped on. We had driven about three kilometres when I saw the gendarmes.

"Whoa!"

I stopped. One of them asked me, "Where are you going?"

"I'm going where the other people are going!" I replied (3).

"Do you have a military pass?"

"Yes, I do."

"Give it here! Let's go see the *starosta*!" (4) The gendarmes placed me in their wagon and we set off, stopping along the way at a roadside tavern where they drank beer by the jug.

"How is it," I asked the gendarmes, "that many of the reservists have already left here, the ones that I know, but yet I'm being taken to see the *starosta*?"

"They left by a different way."

"What kind of different way?" I wondered.

We arrived at the station in Zolochiv and went immediately to see the *starosta*. It was lunch time and he was not in his office but he returned at about three o'clock. I sat on a chair beside a table. The gendarme spoke. "Sir, we are bringing you this reservist whom we found going to Brazil."

The *starosta* put out his hand and said, "Give me your orders."

"I don't have them," I replied.

[To the gendarme] "He doesn't have his orders. Why did you bring him here?"

"He belongs to the army," said the gendarme. "We found him when we were on patrol."

As I sat and listened to this conversation I thought to myself that maybe this would not be so bad after all.

"Where are you going?" the *starosta* asked me.

"To Brazil. My father, my family and me" I said. "We're all going because there is no work here. My father sold his house, his field. There's nothing here for me any more."

"Your father didn't give you any money?"

"No," I said. "He only had a little left for himself. He paid off his debts, his taxes for two years. He only had a little left."

"You can go to the manorial farm (5) for work."

"They don't need any workers on the farms!"

"Whoever wants to work will find work!"

"Of course I want to work and I am looking for a job."

"Bah! You may be on [military] leave. But you are not allowed to run away."

"Sir, I'm not running away! I have permission to leave. I asked, my father asked, the reeve asked and you signed the papers."

"Take him to the magistrate!"

"Sir! Please do not do this to me! Nor to my 63-year old father and the young children, there are four of them, and my stepmother. My father is not well. Without me he won't survive in Brazil!"

Nothing helped. I was taken to the magistrate. Spending the night there, one of the administrators came to see me at eight o'clock the next morning and questioned me... I told the gendarme that I would rather be working than sitting here and so I found a job as a street sweeper. It kept my thoughts occupied and I even earned 30 *kreuzer*. I spent a week under detention by the police. My wife went to the *starosta* in tears, saying, "They took my husband and I don't know where he is! A week has passed already and I haven't seen him! What is going on?!"

The *starosta* said to her, "He will be released. I will write a letter to the commune (6) so that they will watch him so he does not try to flee a second time."

 Сим кінчимо. Прощайте! Ждіть від нас,
Звісток, як нам заблисне ліпший час.

And so I was released. When the gendarmes took me to the *starosta*, my father and the rest of the family ended up leaving for Brazil, taking with them all of the baggage. I was left with only the clothes on my back and winter was coming. We were separated without even so much as a goodbye. My wife did not go with them. She said that if her husband was not leaving then neither was she, and returned to her village with her brother.

Where would we go? What would we do? We no longer had anything of our own and my wife, who was from another village, had gone to stay with her family. When I arrived there my mother-in-law started crying and said, "Children! My children! Where will you go now?" My brother-in-law's wife was very good and she gave us some advice. "Don't worry," she said. "God is good. He will help."

What was I to do now? As the son of a farmer I could not go to the Jew and work as one of his labourers. I spent day and night thinking about what to do. Oh, God! You know me and my intentions! You know what they are! My poor old father! The little children! What were they doing now? I wanted to help them but we were separated and I might never see them all again. Even though I was prevented from leaving, I'll try again! Maybe this time I will be lucky. I want to emigrate...

...The next day I went to see the notary in the village who sent away for a steamship ticket for me. I gave him the ten *rynski* but when the ticket was delivered the next week, it went to the reeve instead. As I was coming out of church on Sunday, the reeve called out, "Pavle, come and see me." I did as he requested.

"Did you pay ten *zoloti rynski* for a ship ticket?" he asked. With some quick thinking I replied, "Uh, it must have been my father who did this. When he was at Nodari's he must have left the money for a ticket for me." At that moment I learned that if you want your enemy to find out your secret, you need only tell your best friend. I could not trust anyone. What would I do now? I was found out again! Wait another half-year? What if I get caught? And all around me the people are asking if I am leaving for Brazil or not.

I had made my decision. I would not emigrate after all but stay here and look for work in the village or the city. It was then that I found out about another transport [of emigrants] which was being prepared...

...People were getting ready to leave. There were so many emigrating. This time I would tell no one of my plans. My wife and I went to the train station in Zarvanytsia and purchased two tickets to Lviv. We boarded the train and left, travelling from Lviv to Stryi where we waited about eight hours before continuing on to Udine, Italy. I had no travel documents at all but was able to avoid the officials. I could finally breathe easier. We spent a whole week in Udine. The leader of the transport had a lot of formalities with so many people in the group. It was here that we

A view of the city of Santos, the state of São Paulo's largest port.

met an interpreter named Bazylko. He could have been a Ukrainian because he got on very well with our people. He joked and laughed with everyone and advised us on how things were done. I asked him about my father. He told me that he had been here but had already left for Brazil. I wondered if I would ever be able to find him again.

We were at sea within a week, boarding the ship on December 8, 1895 and arriving in Brazil on January 1, 1896. It was three o'clock in the afternoon when we came to the immigration barracks in Pinheiro. We would spend a total of four months there. It was May 1st when we arrived in Prudentópolis. Our people had been sick on board the ship but it was much worse in the barracks in Pinheiro. Five, eight, as many as ten people were dying everyday, especially the children. Very few of the younger people survived beyond the barracks. You cannot imagine the sobbing of these five or ten mothers who lost their children in a foreign land, wringing their hands and weeping for these lost lives. The funerals were performed as they could, without a priest, but the cantors Pankevych and Trach would sing the funeral songs and recite Psalm Fifty.

We were fed well, thanks to the Brazilian government, as well as if we were *pany* (7). Some of the people, however, were not satisfied. Boredom set in and they had nothing to do. They talked about their experiences in leaving the old country. Very few had a trouble-free adventure. There were all kinds of stories and much exaggeration. There were some more religious people, like Messrs. Hladky and Dêgan, who sang hymns and performed Sunday matins and vespers.

And so the time passed. The barracks were located close to the train station and there were several *vendas* which served drinks, especially the local Brazilian variety. Some of the people were more frugal than others, they saved their money and did not waste it on unnecessary things. They knew that our situation was so uncertain here. There were others, however, who were in the venda and sipping as soon as it was daylight...

...One day a Brazilian man came to the station with what was for some a very dangerous game. It was a kind of wheel with the images of the sun, moon and stars painted on it. He said to put money here, here, here. The people did, he spun the wheel and we played. Some won, more lost and the fellow just made money! One of the men lost hundreds. He only laughed. And if one of us noticed and suggested that he leave the game alone, it was only a waste of words...

Ivan Dêgan (fourth from left) and his family, linha Inspetor Carvalho, near Prudentópolis.

When we arrived at the barracks, I again asked Bazylko about my father. He replied, "He was here but left about three days ago."

"Please," I said, "perhaps you know where he went? I could write a letter to try and contact him."

"You write a letter and I'll address it for you." I wrote a letter to my father, Bazylko addressed it as he said and took it to the post office. Nothing came of it. There was no reply.

We had not been at the barracks in Pinheiro for very long when a Brazilian priest came to see us, he served a mass and christened some children. There was a chapel, bell tower, a hospital building and two kitchens with long marble tables, benches and a staff to keep things in order. They washed the floors and cooked the meals for the people. Coffee, buns and white bread were served in the morning. The afternoon and evening meals consisted of meat, rice and beans. Most of the people were satisfied knowing that meat was eaten in the old country only on Easter or, by chance, if you had a sick chicken. They even gave us soap for washing our clothes. But there were others who threw down their plates calling out in disgust: "Do you think I'm going to eat such mash?"

The Germans spent a few days here and then left for Santa Catarina. The Italians did the same, resting and then continuing on to São Paulo. The weather was so hot. We waited for our trip to Paraná. One or two of the men and their families went to the coffee plantations, the *fazendas* (8). The people were tired of waiting any longer and so others left too. When it was time to leave, our Polish-speaking friend accompanied us to Prudentópolis as an interpreter because the immigration official did not understand our language nor did we understand his.

A Ukrainian Catholic cemetery, near Prudentópolis.

There had been so many problems and yet we had still not arrived at our final destination. There were troubles in Udine, with Nodari and then Bazylko, and there were so many additional costs. Nodari wanted us to pay for another train ride. He insisted that we pay and so we did. There were six families who were left without any money. I do not know how many times I heard Bazylko translate Nodari's words, "If you don't pay, you don't go. You will be sent back to your village at the cost of the community." And so the people begged us to lend them money. They said, "Have mercy on us, help us, they are going to send us back to our village. To what? To whom? We've already lost everything during the trip to Udine…"

Our people, many of them so good-hearted, lent money to those in need so that they would not be sent home. Bazylko then told us that the steamship companies would transport families for free but single men and women would have to pay 75 *zoloti rynski*. How would the widows, widowers and the young men and women afford this? Many of them did not have that kind of money and so they also risked being denied departure. At times, some of the older people would pay the passage for a single young man, knowing him to be honest and upright and perhaps hoping that one day he might be a future son-in-law. As for the rest, Bazylko did look after them. He said, "I will give you some papers to show that you are married couples with families so that you too will be transported for free." No one was sent back! He also helped everyone exchange their money for the Brazilian currency.

We left the barracks in Pinheiro and boarded a train bound for Santos (9). From there we travelled for three days on a small steamship to Paranaguá and then by train to Curitiba. Within a few days we were continuing on to Ponta Grossa, sleeping on the wagons and arriving in Prudentópolis three days later. We broke branches and bamboo and made little huts to provide shelter from the rain…

There was a chapel, bell tower and two *vendas* here. The storekeeper, Mr. José Durski, was a real character. Almost immediately he began bringing in all kinds of goods. The Brazilians brought in corn, beans, salt pork and other provisions but their supplies were quickly exhausted because there were so many people here. The food was in such demand that at one point you had to pay ten *mil reis* for a quart of unshelled and wormy beans. People were arriving everyday. Goods were being brought in from Ponta Grossa and Curitiba and our people would often meet the *carroças* when they arrived at Durski's *venda* with the supplies.

One day Bazylko said to us "Under orders of the immigration official, you are being asked to construct barracks from branches of bamboo which will serve as a hospital. So many of the people are sick and infirm, especially the pregnant women, and there is no place to care for them." Many of the women became ill and died during the winter when the rains came. Their children, if they survived, were taken in by the Brazilians who liked the light-skinned babies of our people very much. Some of the men also worked on building houses and still others on road construction. They were paid three *mil reis* daily. The money itself was not paid out but the wages were recorded in a book which the people would take to the *venda* and have their purchases deducted from the total.

There were some men who did not want to work at all. Still having some of the money they brought with them, they went to the city where they loafed around, drank and called out, "Why should I go to work cutting down those big trees? Give me a *chácara*! I'll work there but not on the roads!" This was the problem. There were delays in measuring out all of the *chácaras* which were claimed as soon as the engineers surveyed them. Their distribution proceeded fairly orderly. Those with their *chácaras* would not have to spend more than ten days per month on road or any other government work.

The government work lasted until the end of the year. But what now? With no income, the people had no money, nothing to eat, nothing. The settlers were poor and it was even worse for those in the barracks, a few of whom were drinking up their money. Those with some items of value, especially the women, sold kerchiefs, tablecloths, towels, ribbons—whatever they could—in order to buy some food to keep their children and themselves from starving. Some people gave their children away to the Brazilians. Many went out in search of work, travelling as far as 50 miles or more and taking whatever jobs they found. They were often given animals such as cattle or horses for payment.

The immigration officials and their assistants began sending the people out to their *chácaras*. If not enough of them had been measured out, then half-*chácaras*, located closer to the town, were given. This is how our colony of Nova Galícia received its settlers. Mr. Durski, who operated a *venda* in town, built another one in Nova Galícia as more and more people settled here. Soon after he was purchasing erva mate from the people who would carry it on their backs for miles to the store. There were no proper roads or bridges but as soon as they were constructed, Mr. Durski began sending out a wagon to collect the bags of erva mate from the settlers…

…There were hundreds of little huts and shelters in the immigration barracks in Prudentópolis. The immigration official conducted things very well, distributing *chácaras* to the families and suggesting to the others that they get married so as also to claim some of the land (10). The *chácaras*, at that time, were given only to married people. Some of the immigrants took his advice and got married but with no priest here, you had to travel some six miles to Imbituva to the Brazilian church. One of our priests, Father Mykhalevych and his wife, arrived on the very day of Corpus Christi but he did not serve a mass, hear confessions nor perform marriages. A second priest, Father Nykon Rozdolsky, arrived about a month later and took care of all of these duties but stayed for only a few months before going to Rio Claro. Father Voliansky arrived on the day of the Presentation of the Blessed Virgin Mary and although everyone wanted him to stay with us, he too had to leave…

…The people began discussing what they could do in order to make a formal request for a priest to be sent to Brazil. While some had already arrived, they stayed with us only briefly before leaving. The settlers did not even know when the holy days were, couples continued to travel to Imbituva to get married and it was coming to the point where we would be tied to the Brazilian parish there if we did not have our own priest. Some of the more enlightened settlers began meeting and discussing what to do…

...One of my neighbours, having been in the city one day, brought a letter from the post office and asked me to read it for him. He told me that he met Ivan Dêgan there who said that he had written a letter [to the old country] to request a priest. The letter was sent on January 25, 1897. I knew Dêgan from the voyage over. He was an honest, enlightened man and I wanted to talk with him in order to find out more. When the opportunity came for us to speak, I asked: "Did you really send for a priest?"

"Yes I did," he replied.

"How could you ask for a priest when conditions here are so terrible?"

"It was exactly these conditions which prompted me to make the request."

I thought about Dêgan's words for a long time. I know them to be true. I can see the poverty here. I see the Brazilian fields, the people clearing and burning off the land, sowing beans, pumpkin and corn... This is only the beginning for them but it is such hard work. What will be in our future if we do not have our own priest?

...A similar question must be asked in regards to our Ukrainian youth. What about them? There are about 10,000 of us here in Brazil and not one school. What will become of the next generation? Ignorance! Only ignorance! Schools are needed desperately, especially in the colonies where most of our people have settled. Nova Galícia, for example, has a population of 52 families. The priest knows very well that we need a school here. Our Mr. Hladky has told us to look for someone who would be able to teach the children. We selected Oleksa Huk.

How could we build a school when everyone was living in such poverty? No one had horses or wagons with which to bring in the building materials such as wooden timbers and stones for the foundation. Somehow we managed. I remember one of the men saying, "We will carry everything on our backs if we have to, just as a bird carries twigs in its mouth in order to build a nest." And so it was that God helps those who help themselves. The work began. Some broke stones, others cut wood and the people carried everything on their backs from as far as two kilometres away. Those on their way to church or to the city would also carry a stone, two, or as many as they could. The young, old and the children all helped in bringing the material. The work was hard, especially for the women, but their contribution is just as important. A wagon was purchased to make the work a little easier and even though they had to push and pull it themselves (there were no horses) it was much better for everyone. Fedir Moskal was the carpenter and he was assisted by Brother Horoshchuk.

■ ■ ■

Now to finish my story. As I have already told, my family and I were preparing to leave for Brazil when I was apprehended by the gendarmes and taken to the *starostvo* (11) and from there to the police. I was released after a week's detention but my family had emigrated without me. My wife stayed behind, returning to her village to the home of her parents. I still wanted to emigrate and to find my family in Brazil. My father was old and in poor health. My brother Hrynko was sick. My sister Nastia was only 15 years old. My stepmother was young and healthy but there were young children—Ivan was six, Kyrylo was five and Marunka was only three. It never left my thoughts that my family was somewhere in a foreign land. So far away from here. And what were they doing? My father had put all of his hope in me. We had been separated, broken apart so hopelessly that we were not even able to say goodbye.

I had to go. And it was with fear that my wife and I left. I had no passport and no money. I asked continually about my father in every place we stopped along the way. I was told that he had been there but had since left. I always hoped that I would be able to find him.

When we arrived in Prudentópolis, I asked about my family among the transports of immigrants which had arrived earlier but none of them were there. I asked our friend Bazylko if he knew where my father's transport had settled. He named a few places which meant nothing to me, I wrote the letter and he addressed it and sent it off. It was all in vain. Nothing came of that letter. A year passed. Then two. I continued to search for my father. There was never a day or night that passed when I did not think about him and wonder where he was. I asked everyone but no one knew. I often saw my wife in tears. I knew why. She too had missed everyone. She said that we should have taken my brother Vasyl with us but it would have been impossible when we ourselves had to escape like criminals. As far as I knew, Vasyl wanted to become a miller and probably would not have emigrated.

It was a joyous day when our priest arrived. It had been two years since anyone had heard the word of God. A man from a neighbouring village in the old country, Fedko Gavansky, had come to the service. He had been working in Curitiba and stopped here on his way back to Prudentópolis. As the people were talking amongst themselves afterwards, he asked if there was anyone here from his village. Someone told him that there were two families from Koropets, Mykhailo Sukmanovsky and Pavlo Muzyka.

"No," Gavansky said. "That's not possible. Muzyka was not able to leave."

"That's true," he was told, "but later he was able to emigrate. He's now living in Nova Galícia. His wife was here at church today."

"Show me," said Gavansky. "I don't know her."

The people found my wife and introduced her to Gavansky. He then came to see me. What joy and gladness! We spoke for a long time and he told me all about my family here in Brazil. He said that my father's transport was supposed to settle in the colony of Castelhan but the area was hilly and the people did not want to live there. Other settlers told them that it was not a good place to live and so they escaped under the cover of darkness.

"I found a job and stayed in Curitiba. Your father bought a *chácara* in Tomas Coelho (our people called this Moskvália). Your sister Nastia has a job working for a family. Your father is doing well amongst the old Polish and Prussian colonists. Those settlers were good people and helped out the poor ones."

Gavansky spoke further: "I am thinking of moving here to the colony, to be among my own people and closer to my church and priest. When I arrived here, I spent some time at your father's place because it was located along the way. When I return to the city, I'll stop in again and tell him that you are here because he misses you so much. He doesn't know that you are in Brazil. He thinks that you remained in the old country, living poorly and working in the service of others."

"Good, Uncle (12)," I said. "Tell Father that I really want him to come here so that I can see him again." Gavansky left. It was not long after that my father came to see me. Such joy, such happiness and so much talking! He told me that it was good where he was living but the people were not Ukrainians. If he were able to sell his land, he would move here to Nova Galícia to be with me. My father stayed for about a week and then left. He told me all about the family including the sad news that my brother Hrynko had died in Curitiba.

My stepmother and sister came a short time later because my father did decide to sell his land and move here. This was such a happy time for us all. My neighbour was selling his *chácara* at this time and so we bought it. My father was old and infirm, the children were young and we would have to help. I had enough food for us all. Soon after my sister got married. Within a year, my father died. The children were young but my stepmother was a hard-working woman and bought a second *chácara* shortly after. We were happy living here together.

About a year later, I received a letter from my brother Vasyl in Germany. I did not understand why he had left Galicia but he explained it in his letter. He wrote that now, at the age of 24, he was trying to get a passport. He wanted to go to America. Not wanting to work for the Jew any more, he studied and became a miller. He planned to go to America but it was discovered at the pier that he was short of money—ten *zoloti rynski*—and he was not allowed to leave. He ended up going to Germany to look for work. There is a law there that says that foreigners cannot work for longer than a year. You would be sent back. His year was up and he did not know what to do but asked me about Brazil.

I wrote him back and told him clearly about the problems and difficulties here. But he missed us all so terribly and, like me, decided to come. He worked on the railroad for two years. He saved a few hundred *mil reis*, bought a *chácara* and got married. João Pedro Ditzel needed someone for his mill and so Vasyl found work right away. He worked there for a whole year. Having a river on his *chácara*, he also built a mill of his own. He made a good living and has land for his children.

Our friend, Mr. Gavansky, did as he said. He moved to Nova Galícia, bought a *chácara* and is doing very well. He lives close to the church.

74

ENDNOTES

CHAPTER ONE
ABOUT FREE LANDS

1. *Mandioca* (manioc in English) is the Portuguese name for the cassava root. It is widely cultivated in Brazil and, in various forms, is a staple in the Brazilian diet. Its taste is similar to that of a potato.

2. The Austrian currency consisted of the gulden (Ukrainian, *zolotyi rynskyi*, pl. *zoloti rynski*) and the kreuzer (Ukrainian, *kraitsar* or *kreitser*). Beginning in 1857 one gulden contained 100 kreuzer. In 1892, a new currency was introduced while the old one remained in circulation. In the new currency one crown (Ukrainian, *korona*) contained 100 hallers (Ukrainian, *helery*). From 1892 until 1900 when the old currency was withdrawn from circulation, one gulden equalled two crowns and one kreuzer equalled two hallers. In 1895, according to Oleskiv's information, one Canadian dollar was equal to two-and-a-half *zoloti rynski*.

3. The state of Paraná was closed to settlement by the Brazilian government in an attempt to direct new immigrants to the coffee plantations of São Paulo and Espírito Santo.

4. The St. Raphael Society was founded in 1892 in Turin, Italy. Its work was praised but at the same time there were criticisms that the Lviv affiliate was not protecting the emigrants as it should have. For further information on the Society, see *Batkivshchyna*, 1 (13) February 1896.

5. The Hutsuls (*hutsuly* in Ukrainian) are one of three Ukrainian peoples inhabiting the northern slopes of the Carpathian Mountains.

6. A type of gruel made from cornmeal (also called *lemishka*, *mamalyga*).

7. The botocudos (from the Portuguese *botoque* meaning wooden plug) are a South American Indian tribe living chiefly in the forests of southeastern Brazil. The name alludes to the tribal custom of wearing wooden plugs in the ears and lips.

8. The *morg* was a traditional unit of measure in Austria. In Galicia, one *morg* was equal to 0.575 hectares (somewhat more than an acre). Its size varied slightly depending on the region. The *morg* would be further divided into *sazhni* (pl.), one *sazhen* being equal to 3.596 square metres.

9. The *mil reis* is a former Brazilian currency. It was replaced by the *cruzeiro*. Brazil's new currency is called the *real* (pl. *reais*).

10. In addition to the information provided by Hempel and Siemyradzki, numerous warnings about the emigration to Brazil were published in the Galician press. See, for example, *Batkivshchyna* 16 (28) February 1894. This article discusses further the sending of the immigrants against their will to work on coffee and cotton plantations.

CHAPTER TWO
ABOUT EMIGRATION

1. In the village house, the top of the clay oven provided a very comfortable and much-coveted place to sleep. The clay, having been warmed by the fire inside, would retain the heat for several hours and offer a good night's sleep.

2. Parania was a popular Christian name among Ukrainian women. It is the diminutive form of Paraskeva.

3. While Oleskiv himself did not visit Brazil, other members of the Galician intelligentsia travelled to South America and wrote about their findings in the press. See, for example, *Batkivshchyna*, 1 (13) February 1896, 16 (28) February 1896 and 1 (13) September 1896 for detailed reports.

4. See Chapter One, note two.

5. In the 1 (13) April 1894 issue of *Batkivshchyna*, the St. Raphael Society issued a warning for the people not to emigrate to Brazil for this very reason. The 200 *zoloti rynski* which they were required to have with them was not enough to purchase land and therefore they would be forced into work on the plantations.

6. Numerous reports in the Galician press confirm Oleskiv's information about the unscrupulous nature of the agents. What follows are some selected examples:

As reported in the 1 (13) April 1 1894 issue of *Batkivshchyna*, subagent Hrynko Petrychka from Pechenia began calling himself Count von Góral after getting his emigration information from Udine. He was visited by some "30 to 40 people daily from the Peremyshliany and Bibrka counties, charging them a 25 kreuzer port tax which earned him several hundred *zoloti rynski*...even enticing the people by claiming that the son of Emperor Rudolph lived there and wanted everyone to come." Petrychka was eventually jailed for fraud.

A report from *Batkivshchyna*'s 16 (28) May 1896 issue states that some agents were going through the countryside around Rohatyn and showing steamship tickets with the picture of the Austrian Emperor, saying that it was his wish that the people go to Brenzolia where the land is free.

It was reported in the 1 (13) November 1896 issue of *Batkivshchyna* that Martyn Gergel from Leskiv, Sokal county, fleeced the peasants of 1,715 *zoloti rynski* within a two-week period. He sent 425 *zoloti rynski* to the agent in Hamburg and kept the rest for himself. He was required to return the money, fined 100 *zoloti rynski* and ultimately sentenced to jail.

Agents Mieczysław Bazylewicz and Antoni Podolski were being investigated by the gendarmes for their involvement in the emigration movement from Buchach county. As reported in *Svoboda*'s 22 January (3 February) 1898 issue, the villagers went to see them in such numbers "as if they were going to the river for the blessing of the water on Yordan." They were agents from Hamburg and were sending people to Paraguay on the pretense that the Paraguayan Emperor's wife was giving each emigrant 100 *morgs* of land, several cattle, unlimited firewood and free passage. Many people gave them deposits for their tickets. They were sentenced to six months in jail for their fraudulent activities.

7. Silvio Nodari was an Italian steamship subagent in Udine infamous for his crimes against the emigrating Ukrainian peasants. He would consistently overcharge the people for their steamship tickets and abandon them after he received the money. According to a report in *Batkivshchyna* in January 1896: "Afterwards, when the people asked for his help, he now says that he is sick." In another account the following month it was stated that Nodari and his brother Luigi had bilked the emigrants of 20,000 lira (about 9,500 *zoloti rynski*). *Batkivshchyna* regularly ran articles, letters or editorials with titles such as "Beware of Nodari" and "Protect Yourself." Previous to this, a criminal inquiry had been launched against the brothers in 1895 as a result of charges they had bilked 23 Galician peasants of 3,657 lira (about 1,738 *zoloti rynski*).

CHAPTER THREE
THE FIRST TO ARRIVE

1. The emigration to Brazil was marked with disaster in early 1891 with the sinking of the steamship "Utopia" en route from Naples to New York City and thence to Rio de Janeiro. It was reported in the March 29 (April 10), 1891 issue of the newspaper *Batkivshchyna* that it had 700 Ukrainian emigrants and a crew of 60 on board. There were no survivors.

2. Many emigrants to Brazil also departed from the German port of Bremen. F. Missler, one of Bremen's best-known steamship agents, directed many Galicians to Brazil.

3. This is a reference by Pacevicz to the political turmoil in Brazil following the deposition of Emperor Pedro II in 1889 and the establishing of a republic.

4. Ilha das Flores, literally "Island of Flowers," was Brazil's equivalent to Ellis Island. It is located in Guanabara Bay, north of the city of Niteroí in the Municipality of São Gonçalo.

5. Two-and-a-half *mil reis* was approximately one dollar. See also Chapter One, note nine.

6. The *carroça* (pl. *carroças*) is a type of horse-drawn Brazilian farm wagon. It is still widely used in the rural areas of the Brazilian South.

7. *Shakra* (pl. *shakry*), from the Portuguese *chácara*, is a Ukrainian-Brazilian term coined and used by the immigrants to mean farmstead. In contemporary Brazilian Portuguese, *chácara* also denotes a country house. A *shakra* was a land parcel consisting of ten *alqueires* (the *alqueire* is a Brazilian land measure equal to 24,000 square metres) or about 44 *morgs* (25 hectares) in size. Because of the numerous delays in measuring out the *shakry*, the Ukrainian men and boys often helped the surveyors in their work. At this time the price of a *shakra* was 372 *mil reis* paid over ten years.

8. The *foice* was a type of scythe used by the settlers for clearing land.

9. The quart (*kvarta*) was a Galician measure of volume for dry goods. One quart equalled 0.96 litres.

10. *Paska* (pl. *pasky*) is a rich, round Ukrainian Easter bread of varying sizes, decorated with elaborate dough ornaments and blessed by the priest on Easter Sunday.

11. Father Nykon Rozdolsky was one of the first Basilian missionaries in Brazil, arriving from Galicia in July 1896 and serving in Prudentópolis, Rio Claro and Serra de Tigre. He was actively involved in these communities and was instrumental in the building of their churches and schools. Rozdolsky died prematurely in November 1906.

CHAPTER FOUR
OUR BEGINNINGS IN RIO CLARO

1. See Chapter Three, note ten.

2. Herba (also erva mate), sometimes called Paraguayan tea, is widely cultivated in Brazil. Its leaves, dried, ground and steeped in boiling water, are used to make *chimarrão*, a popular drink.

3. The Ukrainians of Galicia in the late nineteenth century called themselves *rusyny*. The Poles called them *Rusini*. This has been rendered in English as Ruthenian. Potoskei uses this term exclusively in reference to Ukrainians.

4. See Chapter Three, note six.

5. The newspaper *Batkivshchyna* regularly contained reports about the delays and problems which the emigrants faced as they waited to board the steamships in Italy. Problems with passports, counterfeit or invalid steamship tickets and insufficient money for the journey were all cited in the newspaper's (16 (28) March 1894 issue. It was further reported that there were 200 Galicians stranded in Italy and practically dying of starvation because they had neither the means to continue on to Brazil nor to return to Galicia.

6. See Chapter Two, note seven, for further information on Silvio Nodari.

7. *Pin'ory* (sing. *pin'or*) is the Ukrainian-Brazilian version of the Portuguese *pinheiro* (pl. *pinheiros*), the name of the Paraná pine tree (Araucaria augustifolia). The tree, which is native to Brazil's southern regions, grows up to 130 feet high, attains diameters of up to six feet in maturity and is marked with its distinctive crown of upturned branches. The early settlers tell that the *pinheiros* were so large that their uprooted stumps left a hole in the ground the size of a house. A similar story tells of six grown men, holding hands and attempting to encircle the trunk of a full-grown *pinheiro*, who could barely reach around it.

8. See Chapter One, note one.

9. Manioc flour.

10. *Mnohaya lita* (literally "Many Years") is a Ukrainian song of well-wishing, congratulation or felicitation, sung on festive and solemn occasions.

11. *Venda* is the Portuguese word for grocery store. It was widely used in the speech of the immigrants.

CHAPTER FIVE
MEMORIES FROM THE FIRST WAVES OF EMIGRATION

1. Cottagers, called *khalupnyky* in Ukrainian, were landless peasants. They possessed no garden or field for cultivation, only their house, and typically worked as craftsmen, tradesmen or labourers on the farms or estates of others.

2. Aleksey (also Oleksa) Shcherban was one in a long line of unscrupulous steamship agents and subagents (he himself was a subagent) operating in East Galicia at this time. The immigrants referred to him sarcastically in Portuguese as *o bom ruteno* (the good Ruthenian). This transport, Shcherban's third, arrived in Rio de Janeiro from Galicia in a record time of 30 days (January 4 to February 3, 1896). Most voyages took two to three months from departure to arrival.

   Reports of Shcherban's misconduct were a frequent feature in the Ukrainian press. It was reported in the 1 (13) February 1896 issue of *Batkivshchyna* that Shcherban had bilked the 206 Ukrainian emigrants from Hotzailuk's group of 1,700 *zoloti rynski*. When he was taken to court and ordered to return the money, which he did, it was further revealed that he took an additional ten *zoloti rynksi* from each of the people in 99 families who were planning to emigrate to Brazil. Shcherban told the court that these were payments for steamship tickets which at that time were still being distributed (through the St. Raphael Society) for free. He was jailed at the beginning of February 1896 on orders from the state, leaving 11 families from Pidhaitsi who were destined for Brazil stranded in Lviv.

3. Shcherban's office was located at the hotel Zolota Ryba in Lviv in 1895-6. It was at the hotel that the emigrants were subjected to passport control and document inspection, and where they were required to produce the amount of money necessary for the expenses of the journey to Brazil.

4. Three hundred gulden was approximately $120 Canadian dollars.

5. Galicia retained the Julian calendar (also referred to as "Old Style") until 1918. From March 1, 1800 there was a 12-day difference between the Julian and Gregorian calendars and a 13-day difference from March 1, 1900. According to this calendar, Christmas Eve fell on January 6.

6. *Yordan* or *Vodokhryshchi*, the Feast of the Epiphany, is celebrated on January 7 (January 19, New Style). It commemorates the baptism of Christ in the Jordan River and traditionally ends the Christmas season for Ukrainians. On this day, the rites of the blessing of the water are performed. In the European villages, this would usually have been done on the banks of a frozen river or lake. A cross would have been erected from blocks of ice. Following the blessing, the people would return home with some of the water to bless their houses.

7. *Khrystos Voskres* (literally "Christ is Risen") is a traditional Easter hymn.

8. Manioc flour, typically seasoned and toasted.

9. See Chapter One, note five.

10. See Chapter Three, note six.

11. *Pinhões* (sing. *pinhão*) are the nuts or acorns of the *pinheiro*. Often the sole food for the first immigrants in Brazil, they were gathered, roasted, ground into flour and then baked into a bread or cooked into a type of gruel. When roasted, the *pinhões* have a chestnut-like flavour. They are still widely eaten in southern Brazil, collected and prepared by the people themselves when in season, and sold freshly-boiled at roadside stands.

12. *Bethlehem Night*.

13. *Carnaval* is a special time of festivity, European in origin, observed in Roman Catholic countries. It occurs between the Epiphany and Fat Tuesday as a prelude to the self-denials of the Lenten season. *Carnaval* is widely celebrated in Brazil, the most famous of the festivities taking place in Rio de Janeiro.

CHAPTER SIX
IN SEARCH OF A BETTER LIFE

1. *Bugres* is the Portuguese word for Brazilian-Indians.

2. See Chapter Five, note one.

3. Kobrên refers to the Italians as *taliany*, a word of his own creation with elements from both Portuguese and Ukrainian.

4. Vobrazylia was one of the many different versions of the Ukrainian *Brazylia*, meaning Brazil, which was used by the emigrants. See also Oleskiv's account of this in Chapter Two, *About Emigration*.

5. *Spasa* or *Spas*, the Feast of the Transfiguration of the Lord, falls on August 6 (August 19, New Style) and traditionally ended the harvest season. Grain, fruits and honey would be blessed in church on this day. The Feast is also connected with the ancient rite of ancestor worship.

6. This translates from Portuguese as "Gentlemen, who wants to buy oranges, bananas?"

7. "Good afternoon" in Portuguese.

8. The confusion arose from the word *do*, meaning "of" in Portuguese (a contraction of *de* and *o*) but "to" in Ukrainian. In reading the railway sign, the immigrants understood the Portuguese *do Brasil* ("of Brazil") to mean "to Brazil" in their native Ukrainian.

9. The *plakhta* was a type of women's waistline garment. It was a rectangular cloth, typically made of homespun linen, and worn wrapped around the waist.

10. In February 1896, it was reported in *Batkivshchyna* that there were 1,500 immigrants from Galicia living in the immigration barracks in Pinheiro. The surveying of the land in Paraná had not been completed which necessitated their detention. It was further reported that the delays were causing the people to use their money for living expenses at the barracks but even worse were the crowded conditions, the unbearable heat and the inadequate rations of food which they were given.

11. See Chapter Four, note ten.

12. This translates from Portuguese as "They know how to dance well!"

13. This translates from Portuguese as "Eat, eat, it won't hurt you, we all eat the very same thing."

14. Not knowing Portuguese, the immigrants read Curitiba as *Tsuritiba* according to Polish orthography in which the letter "c" is pronounced as "ts."

15. An expression meaning "It's done" or "It's ready" in Portuguese.

16. *Pyrohy*—boiled or baked dumplings filled with potatoes, sour cabbage or groats. *Lemishka*—a type of gruel made with cornmeal. *Holubtsi*—cabbage leaves stuffed with rice, meat or groats. *Borshch*—beet soup.

17. See Chapter Three, note five.

CHAPTER SEVEN
IN THE PATHS OF MANY

1. See Chapter Four, note nine.

2. The *sopilka* (pl. *sopilky*) is a type of flute made from a branch of elder, cranberry or ash with six or seven holes on top. There are several different types of *sopilky*, some with reeds and some without. The sound is shrill and high-pitched.

3. The *caboclos* are civilized Brazilian Indians of pure blood.

4. *Parastas* in Ukrainian.

5. *Kościół* is the Polish word for church, used here with specific reference to a Roman Catholic church.

CHAPTER EIGHT
AND FOR THE MEAL PYROHY AND PIRANHAS

1. This is a reference to Antonio Gergoletto, an Italian steamship agent from Udine, whose crimes against the peasant emigrants are legendary. Gergoletto travelled to Galicia, visiting hundreds of villages and introducing himself to the people as Archduke Rudolph Habsburg, the only son of Emperor Franz Joseph of Austria. Habsburg was dead at this time, having committed suicide in 1889. Gergoletto told the people of the wonders of Brazil where everything was free—land, houses, cattle, horses, food—and that money was given for the initial expenses of settling in. In April 1894, it was reported in *Batkivshchyna*: "Gergoletto has fleeced our people most of all. He is a fraud and a cheat." He escaped to Brazil to avoid arrest, leaving his work to his successor, Silvio Nodari, who had an emigration agency in Udine. Gergoletto died in 1894.

2. The family's surname comes from the Ukrainian word *more* meaning sea. Family lore tells of maritime lineage and an ancestry of sailors from where the surname is said to come.

3. Fiume in Italian.

4. This is a Portuguese idiom, *ver navios*, which translates as "to watch the ships go by" with the implication of being left behind.

5. *Se Deus quiser* translates from Portuguese as "If God wills."

6. The *sanfona*, or hurdy-gurdy, is a musical instrument for street music.

7. *Fazendeiros* (sing. *fazendeiro*) is the Brazilian term for plantation owners.

8. A *facão* is a big knife, usually carried in a sheath.

CHAPTER NINE
AMONG OUR PEOPLE IN SOUTH AMERICA

1. See Chapter Five, note 13.

2. *Kapusniak* is a type of sour cabbage soup.

3. This translates from Portuguese as "Good day."

4. *Shche ne vmerla Ukraina* ("Ukraine Has Not Yet Perished") is the Ukrainian national anthem.

5. Karmansky would have been familiar with the Canadian Prairies, having come to Winnipeg in July 1913. He was appointed lecturer at the Ruthenian Training School in Brandon that same year. He returned to Galicia in 1914.

6. See Chapter Three, note nine.

7. *Yide, yide Zelman* was one of the popular and much loved *haivky* or spring song-dances which were performed during the Easter celebrations.

8. *Ne pora!* ("This is Not the Time!") is a song of national character written by Ivan Franko.

CHAPTER TEN
WE COOKED THE CHICKEN SEVEN TIMES

1. *Bagunça* translates from Portuguese as disorder, confusion or noisy feasting. It can also mean "high jinks" of any kind.

2. The *starosta* or matchmaker was one of the most important figures in the Ukrainian wedding. In one of his first and most important roles, the *starosta* traditionally accompanied the bridegroom to the home of his betrothed to request formal permission for the marriage to take place (the bride would be assisted by a *starosta* of her own). He was present throughout the entire wedding celebration, directing the various ceremonies and overseeing that all of the required rites and rituals were being observed. The *starosta* was usually an older man, a relative or close friend of the families or a man of local prominence or importance.

3. The *tsymbaly*, or hammered dulcimer, is a popular Ukrainian folk instrument.

4. *Pinga* (also called *cachaça* and *aquardente* in Portuguese) is a spirit made from fermented sugar cane.

5. The *korovai* was the most important of the Ukrainian wedding breads and held a prominent place within the wedding traditions. It was prepared according to a complex ritual of blessings and songs, elaborately decorated with dough ornaments and flowers and formally presented to the couple during the celebration. In Brazil, a *pinheiro* sapling (affectionately called *pin'orchyk*), decorated with flowers and ribbons, was thrust upright into the *korovai* and carried in procession by the bridegroom's attendant.

6. See Chapter One, note eight.

CHAPTER ELEVEN
LETTERS HOME

1. Osyp, to whom the letter is addressed, is Veltchevski's brother-in-law (his wife's brother).

2. Mechalovsky was a native of the village of Klebanivka, Zbarazh county, East Galicia.

3. This is a reference by Mechalovsky to a *chácara*. His reference to the distribution of land parcels in Rio de Janeiro is incorrect.

CHAPTER TWELVE
TO FIND MY FATHER

1. From *baba*, the Ukrainian word for grandmother. It is used here in its diminutive form.

2. The Feast of the Assumption of the Blessed Virgin (*Uspennia Materi Bozhoi*) falls on August 15, Old Style (August 28, New Style).

3. The gendarmes addressed Muzêka in Polish. His replies were in Ukrainian. Polish was the official language of local government, administration and business in Galicia at that time. The majority of schools also used Polish as the language of instruction.

4. The *starosta* was the county officer. The term is also used to designate the matchmaker within the traditions of a Ukrainian wedding. See Chapter Ten, note two.

5. A manorial farm is called a *filvarok* in Ukrainian.

6. The commune or *hromada* was a level of local organization or government within rural East Galicia.

7. This is a sarcastic reference to the Polish lords (*pany*) who in the peasants' eyes enjoyed a life of leisure and luxury while the Ukrainians performed their manual labour.

8. The *fazenda* was a large estate, typically for the growing of coffee or cotton, with its own agricultural, economic and social organization. It was a business undertaking, run for profit by its proprietor, the *fazendeiro*, who would enter into contract with tenant colonists on a short-term basis of one to two years. While they could be of varying sizes, a typical Brazilian *fazenda* is about six square miles in size.

9. Santos is the chief seaport of the state of São Paulo.

10. Other reports of the conditions within the immigration barracks in Prudentópolis are contrary to the information provided here by Muzêka. Under the director of colonization, Dr. Ozório Guimarães, there was no organization, inadequate food supplies, delays in the distribution of land and raging epidemics with 30 to 40 people dying everyday. In such conditions and overcrowding, the people were being forced against their will to leave the barracks for the interior. A report by the Vincentian Fathers of the parish of São João Batista in Prudentópolis indicated that those who resisted were forcibly placed inside baskets and transported by mules across the Rio São João. The bridge was then burned so that the immigrants would not be able to return to the city.

11. The *starostvo* was the district captaincy.

12. From *vuyko* (literally uncle), widely used by Western Ukrainians as a form of address, especially when speaking to an older man.

SELECTED BIBLIOGRAPHY

Boruszenko, Oksana. "Ukrainians Abroad: In Brazil," *Ukraine: A Concise Encyclopedia Vol. 2* (Toronto: University of Toronto Press, 1971).

—-. "Do temy nashoho stolittia u Brazylii," *Tsvirkun* 203 (Curitiba: n.p., 1991).

Burko, Valdomiro, OSBM. *A Imigração Ucraniana no Brasil* (Curitiba: n.p., 1963).

—-. *Otsi Vasyliany u Brazylii* (Prudentópolis: Basilian Fathers Press, 1984).

Cipko, Serhii. "The Legacy of the 'Brazilian Fever:' The Ukrainian Colonization of Paraná" in *Journal of Ukrainian Studies*, Vol. 11, No. 2 (Winter 1986), Edmonton.

Gomes, Neonila (ed). *Prudentópolis, Sua Terra e Sua Gente* (Prudentópolis: n.p., 1971).

Haneiko, Valdemiro, OSBM. *Uma Centelha de Luz* (Curitiba: Editora Kindra, 1985).

Lehr, John, Stella Hryniuk and Jeffrey Picknicki. "A Tale of Two Frontiers: Settlement in Canada and Brazil 1891-1914" in *The Estevan Papers* (Estevan: University of Regina, 1995).

Lysa, Natalia. *Ukrainske zhinotstvo u Brazylii*, 1924-64 (Prudentópolis: Basilian Fathers Press, 1964).

Karmansky, Petro. *Mizh ridnymy v Pivdennii Amerytsi* (Vienna: Chaika, 1927).

Picknicki Morski, Jeffrey. "Ukrainians in Brazil," *Generations, Journal of the Manitoba Genealogical Society*, Vol. 14, No. 3 (September 1989).

—-. "Pyrohy and Piranhas: The Ukrainian Immigration in Southern Brazil," *East European Genealogist*, Vol. 4, No. 2 (Winter 1995), Winnipeg.

—-. "Commemorating a Centenary: The History of Ukrainian Settlement in Brazil," *Ukrainian Weekly* (Jersey City, NJ), 5 January 1992, 12 January 1992.

Shymchi, Dorotei, OSBM. *Pershyi miy rik u Brazylii* (Prudentópolis: Basilian Fathers Press, 1983).

Vihorynsky, Irenei, OSBM. *Irasema v istorychnomu rozvytku v 1895-1958 rr.* (Prudentópolis: Basilian Fathers Press, 1958).

Zinko, Vasyl, OSBM. *Ridna shkola v Brazylii* (Prudentópolis: Basilian Fathers Press, 1960).